GOAL SETTING

Key to
Individual
and
Organizational Effectiveness

GOAL SETTING

Key to

Individual

and

Organizational Effectiveness

By CHARLES L. HUGHES

AMERICAN MANAGEMENT ASSOCIATION

Contents

Introduction

THE PSYCHOLOGIST KURT LEWIN ONCE SAID, "THERE IS NOTHING SO PRACTICAL as a good theory." Behavioral scientists have never had any difficulty in developing theories, but applying these concepts of people at work, of employee performance on the job, to real-life business situations has been a continuing problem. What industrial psychologists know—or think they know—is too often far removed from actuality; hence the sizable gap between theory and practice.

Most managers and behavioral scientists do not share each other's world. It is not surprising, therefore, that the researcher cannot translate what he has found into the language of the executive, nor can the executive convey the realities of corporate life to the scientist. Many good ideas about improving the performance of employees fail in actual practice, not so much because the theories are wrong as because we are unable to develop and implement them in a manner consistent with the overall structure and philosophies of a particular organization. And the test of a good theory is its workability in the organizational environment.

Today there are many good theories of motivation, many potentially useful concepts about increasing employee commitment to company objectives and goals. This book is an attempt to synthesize these many eclectic ideas and translate them into terms meaningful to the business manager. To do so we must look not only at the theories themselves but at company practices and management attitudes. This process will bring to light numerous conflicts between theory and application and inevitably point up obsolete thinking and inadequate management behavior.

The test of reality must be applied to both theory and practice. Theories of motivation make sense only if the motivated behavior of both management and nonmanagement employees actually contributes to the ends of the enterprise. Motivation for its own sake is senseless—in fact, impossible. Motivation practices that do not directly or indirectly contribute to achieving organizational goals have no place in management, and by the same token management practices that prevent individual employees from achieving personal goals will in the long run be equally futile.

Just as the apparent conflict between theory and application is often one of narrow perspective, so too is the apparent conflict between the goals of the company and the goals of its individual members. Any attempt at synthesis demands that we identify a common world for all of us who live a great deal of our lives in a search for personal meaning as members of an organization. Both the organization and the individuals that comprise it seek positive goals. In some cases, personal goals are closely related to those of the organization, but in all too many instances people seek ends that cannot be achieved within the corporate framework. The identification of meaningful goals—for both organization and individual—that will effectively influence and support each other is essential to effective performance on the part of the organization and its members alike.

There is much concern today over the need for goals generally: goals for the United States, goals for the cities, goals for corporations and universities, and goals for people, as individuals and as members of these various groups. Too often, however, we find lots of activity but little concern for where it is taking us. Too often we worry about means of transportation without first determining where we want to go. We engage in building and tearing down, making money and spending money, receiving information and giving it, working at jobs day after day without stopping to decide on the goals that those jobs, we hope, will attain. Yet no job in whatever organization has meaning unless it moves us toward a worthwhile goal, unless it helps to achieve the objectives of the organization—and no organization is of any use unless it also helps to achieve the goals of its members. Effective performance thus depends upon the validity of the goals themselves and upon the goal-setting process that is used.

A goal is an end, a result, not just a task or a function to be performed. It is a place in space and time that describes the condition we want to achieve. It is a standard of achievement, a criterion of success, something tangible, measurable, and valuable that we are motivated toward. It is concrete and explicit, definitive and desirable and predetermined. It guides our actions and helps us plan as individuals and as managers. It can be long-range or short-range: Long-range goals help clarify our short-range goals, major goals determine minor goals, and the present is determined by the future— not the past.

We can know what we are as individuals or as a group only after we have first considered what it is we are trying to become. We can know whether what we are doing is absurd only after we have identified the goals we are trying to achieve. We can know the meaning of our individual jobs only after we have recognized the reason for our coming together as an organization. We are nothing more than what we do, and we can become nothing more than what we see ourselves achieving in terms of goals. We are individually responsible for what we are and what we choose to make of ourselves —in short, for our own existence. There is no one to decide everything for us. We cannot know where we are going in our personal or in our work lives until we know where we are all going.

Our activities, then, must make sense against the test of reality. We cannot simply wait like the two characters in Samuel Beckett's *Waiting for Godot* who do not know who Godot is, cannot know when he arrives, and have no idea how long they have been waiting or how much longer they should hold out. Their behavior makes no sense to them, nor does the world they exist in. "Shall we go?" asks the one, in the last scene of the play, and the other replies, "Yes, let's go." But neither moves.

PART ONE

Motivation and Management

Chapter 1

Conflict—Inevitable or Not?

C AN A COMPANY AND ITS EMPLOYEES BOTH HAVE WHAT THEY WANT, OR IS dissatisfaction inevitable for either side?

This question—so often asked today—sums up one of the chief problems facing our free enterprise economic system in an era of growing controls on behavior: how to make the organization and its individual members more effective. The answer would seem to lie in harmony of goals and in a concept of goal setting which will motivate individuals to work together both for the common cause and for personal reasons.

Goal setting is a process for deciding where you want to go. To business executives, it is implicit in what is known currently as "management by objectives." To rank-and-file employees, it is the first step toward job success. Goal setting is often an *iterative* process; that is, it means planning your destination by trying various combinations and permutations of objectives until you find the best possible "fit" for your purpose.

But, if it's a good thing to know where you want to go, it's also good to decide how to get there—after you decide on your goals. In simple terms, you have to know which city you want to reach before you know whether to fly, drive, or both. *Ends determine the means.* It is discouraging, however, how many times people—and companies—start out to do a job before they know what it is they hope to accomplish.

The Organization as the Expression of People

Does the organization set goals? Does it "exist"? There *is* such a thing as the organization—the institution—and it is more than the sum total of the individuals who comprise it. Those who carry management responsibilities shape and influence it markedly, and "the company" reflects ideas and strate-

13

gies and tactics and policies which have stemmed from the president or other key individuals.

If you take all the people out of the organization, it does not cease to exist except in an eventual sense. However, the important thing is that in fact you do take all the people out of it by turnover and it still goes on existing. You take the people out of it from time to time and over a span of years, not all at once, and the organization continues to have a recognizable and identifiable personality which is unquestionably changed by successive managers but which also retains a flavor and a background inherited from those who have gone before. If the chief were to be fired tomorrow, the company would still be an institution with much the same goals and much the same philosophies—at least for quite a long period of time. Some of the institutional characteristics will probably live as long as the corporation does.

Further, if major corporate goals were entirely personal and not institutional, an ego, a great "I," would be always present—with the consequent strong flavor of dictatorship rather than leadership and voluntary association on the part of the individuals concerned. When true institutional goals exist, coupled with a strong personal relationship between responsible leaders and all who must participate in achieving those goals, a better base is established than when the relationship is entirely one of passive acquiescence to a single influential leader.

Anthropomorphic attitudes often serve as a refuge from personal responsibility in connection with goal setting and attainment. There is a mystique about an institution, too, which is more than just the combined efforts, the attitudes and motivations and goals of the men and women who make up the organization at any one time. A political party, for example, is something over and beyond those voters who are presently Democrats or Republicans and considerably more than could be expressed by the leadership of any President. And the United States as a nation is considerably more than the millions of people who are its citizens now. These institutions have a past; they have a framework and traditions derived from that past. The present and the future are dependent upon the individuals who are now or will later be in positions of leadership, but these men are not free of the past. Even the President of the United States is constrained by the Constitution and by our traditions.

All of this means that there are organizational goals which are not just simply the top man's goals, however much he changes and influences them and however much he is responsible for the success or failure of the institution during his term of office.

The Fallacy of Company Omniscience

A few words of caution are necessary, however, about how we communicate with employees about the company. Management cannot persist in deluding itself about the omnipotence and omniscience of the organization.

Sometimes managers will say, "The organization needs . . ." or, "The company feels . . . ," even dissociating themselves from the action or policy in question. Small wonder, then, that employees too often come to believe that the company does actually live and breathe. They remind us of those primitive peoples who assigned human characteristics to things and believed that the chief priest shared powers of the gods that were expressed through his person and personality. In the "primitive" business organization, management speaks to its employees in the same terms: "It is not the company way." "Company survival demands . . ." "We here at the company think . . ." Statements like these are the sign of managers who no longer have a concept of themselves as people but, rather, think of themselves as parts of a humanlike thing.

In biology there is something called "symbiosis," which is the living together of two dissimilar organisms, each continuing to exist only so long as the other does. In the same way, managers can exist symbiotically with their organizations—to such an extent that one wonders whether they would disappear psychologically if separated from the company. And what makes matters worse is that such a concept of the relationship between individual and company is contagious. Hence the "organization man" and the self-searching he has occasioned in management circles of late.

The concept of symbiosis is also found in the psychology of abnormal behavior. Here it is sometimes applied to mother-child patterns in which the child fails to develop an awareness of himself as a separate individual. It is as though mother and child were one; if the mother is removed, the child ceases to exist psychologically. And so it is in business. For the sake of its employees and for its own psychological health as well, management must recognize that it cannot be a mother—or a father. There is no company family. Nor should we fill the organization with people who seek a home at work and a dependent relationship, although in some cases the frustration of their private lives may lead to dedicated productivity on the job.

Human growth or maturity is an endless process of "individuation." Managers have the challenge of being individuals and of arranging the world of work so that all their employees may be individuals.

Science has essentially stopped the physical evolution of human beings, but psychological evolution is just now emerging. And just because the impact of work on people is so overwhelming, the mythology surrounding the organization is potentially dangerous when it distorts employee behavior. It is downright unhealthy to believe that "the company says"! We must always be conscious that, when "management says," actually "a particular individual manager says. . . ."

Integrated Goals and Management Style

The company, then, does not set goals. Only people can do that, although they are influenced by their perception of the company's philosophy. Just as people are the organization, organizational goals are the human expression of human goals. We can and do, however, speak of "company goals" as a convenient shorthand as long as we remain aware that we do not mean the term literally.

To be realistic, it is top management which has the most influence in deciding what will and will not be done; that is, in determining company goals. The style and tone set by these leaders influence the actions of their subordinates.

Regardless of the type of people hired, organization structure and supervisory behavior reflect the leaders' values or others' perception of those values, and managers reward that behavior which correlates with their style and punish that which does not. Hiring goal-oriented people does not assure a high level of goal-oriented motivation; opportunity and incentive to define and pursue goals are offered only if the leaders themselves establish a pattern of goal-oriented behavior. The wellspring of motivation, therefore, is goals as represented in seeable, hearable, and understandable communication from top management.

It is the stated or implied objective of most companies to hire the best employees they can find and attract. However, the dollar value of a job candidate may influence the hiring decision when the salary he asks is more than the company compensation system can allow. The problem is perhaps better understood in terms of goals: Will this candidate achieve results, vital to company success, that will pay his way and add enough to profit? This is admittedly a difficult question to answer, but for a simple reason. We have to know the organization goals the potential employee can be expected to reach, their value to the company, and the effect on profit. Management seldom has this knowledge because the world of work has too many jobs that lack goals which are understood by either manager or worker; often, both fail to recognize the difference between working toward a goal and just performing a task.

This book aims to make the integration of organizational and individual goals well enough understood in concept to be applied by any manager who reads it. It explains how to overcome the traditional error of trying to motivate people to meet objectives that are *not* known. Top management is inescapably responsible for setting company goals; the best-motivated employee must be able to see the value of management's aims or else remove himself or be removed from the company. However, if opportunities for seeking goals are present in the work environment and in the jobs themselves, both motivated and unmotivated people will respond. The capacity for meeting this challenge is broadly distributed in the workforce and will surely emerge.

Chapter 2

Needs, Purpose, and Organization

G OALS DERIVE FROM PURPOSE, WHICH IN TURN DERIVES FROM NEEDS. BUT, YOU may say, where do the goals of my particular company come from? Why *these* goals rather than others? Is there a prime factor which determines the goals of an organization?

Remember that an organization exists only as an expression of the personal goals of its members, past and present, and in large part as an extension of the needs or goals of its leader—the president. In a one-man enterprise, the purpose of the business is the expression of that one man's purpose. In a larger organization, goals become divergently intertwined so that the purposes of many individuals can be and typically are obscured. This purposelessness is usually traceable to lack of direction or uncommunicated direction at the top.

The organization, with the accompanying management system, is the result of the president's or leader's efforts to accomplish the corporation's purpose. It reflects his personality and needs. If he is goal-oriented and cognizant of a purpose, then the organization should be able to achieve both individual and organizational goals—provided the needs of all concerned are truly compatible.

If the president could do everything and know everything himself, he wouldn't need the rest of his organization. He would be all of it. But, in the modern corporation, the leader is neither infallible nor indefatigable and must depend on many other individuals. And, once he adds others to help him achieve his purposes, all must support his (the organization's) purposes; otherwise they don't belong. Yet these other human beings, to exist as individuals, must also serve their own purposes and seek personal goals that meet their needs. This does not mean that the president's purposes and those of his employees are in conflict. Certainly the expression of these purposes may be different, but there is a way, even in today's complex world of industry, to see that they all are served.

The Purpose of Becoming

To know how this is to be done, we must know what these purposes are. In essence, of course, they are *human* purposes of the most basic sort; in fact, there is one purpose which the president and his employees share with all human beings—the purpose of *becoming*. Becoming what? More human; that is, actualizing the human potential for psychological growth.

This idea is expressed many times and in many ways—philosophy, religion, ethics, psychology, common sense—by many people. Some may say, "I just want to be myself"; others may want to "become more tomorrow than I am today." *Being* implies acceptance of personal responsibility and a search for individuality. It is an attempt to answer the question, "Who am I?" to develop and understand one's self, to know who and what one is without depending on name, rank, profession, work, or company affiliation to give meaning to one's existence. And only through one's potential for doing things, using one's abilities, achieving personal goals, can one develop as a human being and learn to be responsible for one's behavior.

Man's purpose, in other words, finds expression in achieving individual goals. In modern as in ancient times, individuals have tried to do this together, for it is through interaction with other people seeking the same purpose that there is hope for *becoming*.

Obviously this is not true just in our business lives; still, we must recognize the important role of work here. Through work, man has the opportunity to be aware of himself in the process of becoming—not just work in an office or plant or even as part of a great corporation, but work in many forms. Another way to achievement and psychological growth is, of course, through participative sports—in fact, most sports provide excellent conditions for growth and achievement, as do personal projects of a creative or challenging nature. Yet do we ever stop to ask why these things are personally satisfying and meaningful while the jobs so many of us spend our lives doing are so dissatisfying? Must work in the corporation be psychologically detrimental to human purpose?

The trouble lies in the negative emotions that the word "work" generally arouses. Work itself can and must have real meaning to the individual. Our problem, then, is this: How can we bring into the work situation that motivation toward goal achievement which is so often expressed at play and during leisure hours? How can employees achieve personal goals at the same time, and by many of the same actions, that they achieve company goals?

Not Profit Alone

One first step toward the required compatibility we have already described: Abandon the idea of the corporation as a mysterious person and understand that it consists of individual people. A next step is recognition of this basic human purpose of becoming which the president and all his employees share. With these two ideas in mind we can proceed to define company purpose.

A survey of top management has shown that few presidents can say what their company purpose is. Many, if pressed, offer statements relating to current products or last year's profits, but these are not corporate purposes. Rather, the president must define the reason for the existence of the company and then communicate it in terms meaningful to other employees—that is, in terms that will indicate how *their* needs as well as his can be served. These terms will spell out the organizational goals which are prerequisites for motivation and achievement.

Company profit *is not a purpose or a goal*—either for the company or for any individual in it, including the president. Profit is, however, an incentive and a means to reach goals and serve mutual needs. It is also a criterion or standard of achievement; it tells employees how well the company has met certain objectives. In the same way, personal profit—that is, the paycheck or year-end bonus or salary increase—is not an individual goal but a standard by which an employee can measure how well he is doing in supporting company goals. It may, of course, be an incentive, too, for merit pay is to the employee what profit is to the manager with balance-sheet responsibility.

A Goal-Setting "Umbrella"

The president's personal goals, we have said, should encompass the organization's goals, broadly conceived. The vice president's personal goals also are closely related to the organization's goals, again by virtue of his location in the hierarchy. But, as we consider individuals at successively lower levels in the organization, their "piece of the action" becomes more specialized, and usually—though not necessarily—their personal goals are more difficult to achieve. Their personal horizons and targets may or may not be as broadly conceived as the president's. It is less likely, however, that their personal targets will encompass as much of the company's targets. Inevitably, opportunity for synthesizing personal and corporate goals decreases as one looks down the organizational ladder. Or, to put it another way, employees at lower levels have relatively less chance to participate in setting organization objectives compatible with their personal goals.

The challenge to modern management is to provide a goal-setting "umbrella" where personal targets can be sighted and reached by individuals at all levels of the enterprise. This is the key to motivation at work, and management must recast its concept of corporate goals in this perspective—integrate the goals of the organization with the goals of its members and make personal goals attainable within the corporate framework.

Humanism is not the only consideration behind such a concept. Clearly, people will seek to satisfy their personal motivation needs. So, if management

1. Makes company goals known to the employees and
2. Provides opportunities for employees to participate meaningfully in meeting these objectives
3. In a way that gives employees a chance for identifying personal goals
4. The motivation to work that results will achieve
   a. Company goals as well as
   b. Personal goals.

Compatability and Achievability

The integration of company and personal goals does not mean that employees must adopt company goals as a replacement for their own. It is equally wrong to assume that the sum of employee goals will equal the company objectives. Such assumptions lead to conflict between management and nonmanagement employees, with each pursuing paths that lead away from achievement.

To force management's objectives (that is, goals not understood) upon other employees, with no opportunities for attaining their own personal goals, leads to dissatisfaction and even to industrial unrest. The union can be looked at as an attempt at salvation by employees who were blocked from satisfying their personal needs—not simply because company goals were different, but because there was no way to reach personal objectives through work. The union is a result of management's failure to recognize that even at the lowest levels employees have personal goals and a need to become.

The futility of unionization is that it cannot change company goals so that they are identical with employee goals and, therefore, cannot satisfy people's need for work that has meaning. A union can, it is true, bargain for pay and conditions of work, but not for the job itself. Typical union activity and attitudes, along with the corresponding management activity and attitudes, block the achievement of personal goals for the very same human beings whose "best interests" both claim to serve.

The goals need not be the same; they must simply be compatible. And compatibility—or, better, achievability—of company and personal goals is possible even though they are different. What is needed to facilitate achievement is a process of goal setting.

Chapter 3

Corporate Planning
And Individual Achievement

T HERE ARE GREAT DIFFERENCES IN THE WAY COMPANIES PLAN, AND CORRESPOND-
ing differences in the effect on individual employee achievement.

Bottom-up planning implies the collection of objectives and plans for reaching them from the grass roots of the organization up through successively higher levels of management until the total package is accumulated. If a satisfactory balance is not evident, then the plans are returned to lower management for adjustment. The company plan is the sum of the individual plans and relies heavily on quantitative data.

Top-down planning starts with company objectives set by top management and distributed to successively lower levels. Each subunit of the organization develops individual plans to meet these predetermined business objectives, and changes are made in the total plan to adjust for individual capabilities. Top-down planning relies heavily on qualitative data.

The principle of contribution to objectives applies in both approaches. Action which does not move the organization toward achievement of goals has no place in the corporate plan, and strategies with a higher ratio of resources used to results achieved have priority over alternatives whose ratio of input to output is lower. Similarly, the principle of management control pertains to both types of planning systems. Each can and must have built-in check points, alternative procedures, and performance criteria.

Top-down planning is often termed bad for employee "happiness" but good for company profits. Contrariwise, the bottom-up technique is said to block company objectives but to be good for morale because of individual participation. The choice is usually assumed to lie between two conditions, both with unpleasant aspects. A company can achieve the one or the other benefit, or neither—but not both unless it is willing to settle for half of each loaf.

This assumption, however, has been predecided by the way the alternatives have been stated. It is not necessarily valid. In fact, we shall attempt to show that

- Top-down planning aids individual achievement (and happiness).
- Bottom-up planning blocks personal happiness (and achievement).

Not that employees want management to prescribe and proscribe their personal objectives. We know they do not—Douglas McGregor explained that long ago. But participation is not, any more than profit, an end in itself, although management may never recover from the lingering myths, arising from the Hawthorne studies, to the effect that participation leads to happiness which leads to productivity.

Freedom from impersonal control is not the same as freedom from personal control—or any control. The dilemma is not which shall we have: happiness or productivity. Participative management cannot be equated with the absence of top-down planning. Further, bottom-up planning is not a sure way to achieve either employee participation in company objectives or employee happiness.

Causes and Effects

The confusion here is in the identification of cause and effect. Lack of employee dissatisfaction *does not* mean good productivity. Bottom-up planning *does not* result in good planning by individuals. Bottom-up planning *blocks* participation, and participation *does not* produce individual happiness. *Cause and effect, in short, have been wrongly identified;* actually, the converse is true in each case. These conclusions can also be stated positively:

- Individual productivity means satisfaction.
- Top-down planning results in good individual planning.
- Top-down planning aids participation.
- Individual achievement produces happiness.

There is no reason to believe that simply being involved is enough to produce motivation or to affect productivity. The only thing that can motivate is the identification of objectives and the expectation of a reasonable opportunity of achieving them.

It is not even correct, basically, to separate individual objectives from company objectives. That is an irrelevant separation because no organization can tolerate objectives whose achievement will not lead to achievement of its own objectives, even though they may encompass customer and society needs. However, if activity in support of company objectives will allow people to reach personal goals, then we have a potentially healthy, happy, and satisfying environment.

Another way of saying it is that the company's basic purpose requires that all activities be directed toward achieving company goals; hence reaching company goals is of necessity an objective of each and every employee. In that process the employee rightly hopes to attain his personal goals—among them, happiness. The key challenge is to achieve company objectives in a manner that will permit the employee to achieve personal goals. Satisfaction and happiness are therefore effects, not causes, and are produced by individual achievement of both personal and company objectives.

Implications for Company Policy and Planning

Without prior knowledge of company goals, individuals do not have the necessary information to set personal work targets that tie into company plans. Thus companies must plan from the top down; otherwise personal objectives will not parallel the company's objectives. And, unless the company's purpose is served as expressed in achievable goals, opportunities for reaching personal goals will no longer exist because the company will no longer exist.

Major business objectives can be set only by people who are in a position to understand the broad, long-range implications of forecast trends and of the various strategies which can be expected to meet the company's requirements. Obviously, top management is the only group of individual employees that can have the necessary information, perspective, and experience. It does not follow, however, that knowledge of overall company plans and the reasons behind them is not needed lower down in the organization. Just as top management needs certain kinds of economic, financial, marketing, and product data to establish objectives for the company as a whole, individuals elsewhere in the organization need to have similar information communicated to them in as much detail as makes sense in light of the targets they must meet. Bottom-up planning without prior knowledge of authorization and goal feasibility is ineffective.

Top-down planning, however, often does not reach far enough down into the organization. What is required is some sort of mechanism that will help to integrate company and personal goals, that will permit and encourage individuals to define the tactics they will use to carry out preselected strategies.

Personal work planning and company planning must coincide, but after the major corporate objectives and strategies have been determined and communicated from the top down. Individual planning can then follow a goal-setting system analogous to the company approach—one that is results-oriented.

There is no satisfactory substitute for working in full harmony to achieve goals that are meaningful not only to the individual but to the company. Participation serves a relevant purpose only when it provides a way to modify company and personal objectives so as to bring them into better alignment. In fact, company policy and procedure must permit this kind of modification in order to fulfill the management goal of using resources—particularly human resources—efficiently.

Management can no longer afford to confuse cause and effect when it considers the problems of employee motivation and productivity. A successful top-down job of setting corporate objectives and communicating them to the levels where the work is actually done is the cause which produces the effect of both individual achievement and company success. Management must recognize that it cannot "participate" an employee into producing.

Toward Improved Planning Effectiveness

The first thing a company should do to improve its planning effectiveness is to identify its corporate purpose. Few organizations do, in fact, have a clear definition—or any statement—of purpose.

An organization's basic purpose, as we have seen, is the reason for its existence, the conceptual foundation of all its objectives and plans. It isn't enough simply to say that the company is in business to "make furniture," for example. That would be shortsighted. Nor is it enough for a statement of corporate purpose just to take cognizance of present customers' needs and those of any other publics it may affect in some way, important though that may be. For, if a business limits its purpose to those customer needs it has traditionally served, it necessarily rules out other such needs. Its planning will therefore focus on objectives that omit many likely opportunities—and individual employees can hardly be expected to pursue goals that they understand to be out of their domain or irrelevant to company objectives.

Take the airlines. They are in more businesses than just plain transportation. What about food and entertainment—or even the vacation-recreation business? Then, too, they have a "business-enhancing" purpose; that is, much of their success depends on aiding other businesses to meet their objectives through facilitating personal communication. Suppose the corporate purpose were stated, in part, as "aiding businessmen in face-to-face communication by transporting people." Suppose, also, that this idea were passed down the line. Might it not affect the job goals and criteria of individual achievement that, say, a supervisor of ground personnel set for himself in unloading baggage? He would then be moving businessmen on their way rather than just following administrative procedures.

As for top management, making it corporate purpose to "serve the face-to-face communication needs of businessmen" surely would clarify the nature of its competition with the telephone (particularly videophone) business. And it might significantly influence company planning in other ways, particularly with respect to marketing and advertising.

Objectives, then, describe goals related to company purpose. Objectives translate purpose into definite targets, with standards of achievement useful to both company and individual. Planned in a top-down pattern, objectives use more qualitative than quantitative data. For example: "Sell X units in the first quarter of the year" prescribes only quantity. In contrast, a qualitative objective might specify: "Capture X percent of the available market no later than April 1." With this indication of quality as well as quantity individual managers and workers will have a lead to follow when setting personal achievement goals. An objective well stated is at least half the answer to reaching it.

What next? What activities must be planned to support objectives, once established? What alternate strategies are possible in the event that factors outside management's control change or planning assumptions prove to be wrong? All these need definition. The question—and the difference between top-down versus grass roots planning—is how individuals down the organizational ladder can make plans that support company purposes and goals if these are not first made unmistakably clear at the top level. How can action be taken to contribute to overall objectives until top management has decided and communicated those objectives?

Overall business objectives must precede individual planning. Top management cannot merely choose goals that happen to be supportable by plans previously made at lower levels. An individual cannot decide where he is going as an individual—regardless of how much he participates in company planning—unless he first knows where the company is going.

Chapter 4

Theories of Motivation
And Management

I T IS POSSIBLE TO ACHIEVE PARTICIPATION—OR, RATHER, INDIVIDUAL INVOLVEMENT —in goal setting by interaction during the planning process. At the foundation of this participation is the company philosophy already described as management by objectives, or *ends*. Contrasting with it is management by controls, or *means*.

If we (1) communicate down the line company goals that have been tentatively set by top management, (2) permit individuals to set the personal goals they tentatively hope to reach, and (3) provide appropriate goal-setting systems in order to (4) facilitate the goal-setting process, then (5) we can have both the necessary top-down direction and grass roots planning. (See Exhibit 1.) The crucial factor is the goal-setting process plus the provision of more than simple participation to get goal interaction. But interaction will be achieved only if management's guiding philosophy permits.

Company philosophy influences employee behavior, which in turn affects the results obtained (Exhibit 2). Managers who practice management by objectives speak and think goals and results. Those who favor management by controls speak and think in terms of *what* people are doing; they care little about *why* they are doing their jobs. Because they look at tasks and not goals, they try to control their employees by close supervision on the job instead of looking to the end results as the more important performance criteria. Yet, if they would think not so much about the doing of a task as about the final outcome, they would be taking advantage of supervisory tactics which would allow them to profit from self-control on the part of their employees.

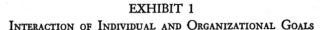

EXHIBIT 1

INTERACTION OF INDIVIDUAL AND ORGANIZATIONAL GOALS

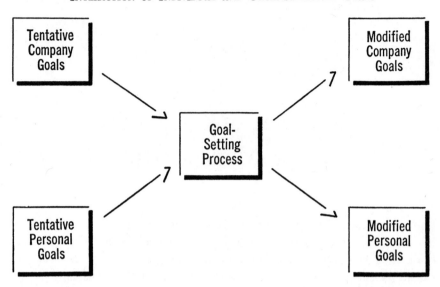

The main point of difference between management by objectives and management by control is that the former, as typified by the results-oriented supervisor, sees contribution to company objectives as more vital than the work itself.

McGregor's Theory X and Theory Y

Behind these two management philosophies are contrasting attitudes about people at work. The late Douglas McGregor described them as Theory X and Theory Y.[1]

Theory X managers assume that (1) people must be coerced into commitment to corporate objectives; (2) they must be controlled constantly by supervisors (otherwise they will not be motivated to work); and (3) they have personal goals that are inherently in conflict with those of the company. *Theory Y* managers believe that people (1) will voluntarily accept corporate goals as a means to their own; (2) do want to work and are capable of self-motivation; and (3) will have personal goals that are compatible with company goals—particularly if they are allowed to participate in goal setting.

The manager or supervisor functions as a mediator between company and

---

[1] Douglas McGregor, *The Human Side of Enterprise*, McGraw-Hill Book Company, 1960

employee goals. To phrase it differently, the supervisor facilitates interaction between the goal setting of one member of the organization and that of the others.

Theory X supervisors perceive their *subordinates'* goals as literally "subordinate" to and naturally in conflict with company objectives. Theory Y supervisors perceive their *fellow organization members'* goals as part of the total of company goals.

Theory X supervisors think goals have been set when each person knows what is expected of him. Theory Y supervisors think goal setting has been accomplished when each person knows what he expects of himself.

Motivation or Maintenance

The inherently human process of becoming means that goal setting in the work situation is a way in which an employee can find out who he is. For the motivation to work is a basic ingredient in human existence,[2] and

EXHIBIT 2
COMPANY INFLUENCE ON EMPLOYEE BEHAVIOR AND RESULTS

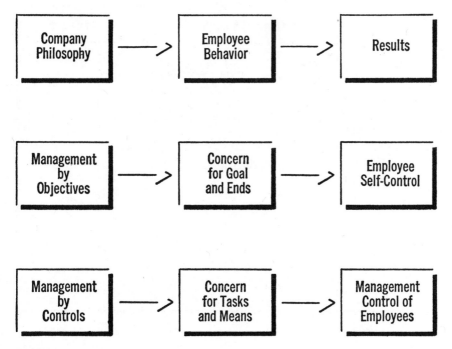

---

[2] Frederick Herzberg, Bernard Mausner, and Barbara Bloch Snyderman, *The Motivation to Work*, John Wiley & Sons, Inc., 1959.

through it the worker satisfies personal needs as he achieves personal goals. And the motivation needs for growth and achievement are a part of everyone's psychological make-up.

People also must maintain themselves physically and feel safe and secure. Thus we speak of *maintenance needs*. Motivation and maintenance needs have distinctly separate characteristics and effects on people at work.[3] Psychologists believe that the lower-order (maintenance) needs must be fairly well satisfied before the higher-level (motivation) needs emerge.[4] Neither set will, however, supplant the other. Both are necessary aspects of behavior and are important in terms of goal setting.

Motivation needs are satisfied through achievement of personal goals. Maintenance needs avoid dissatisfaction through the environment.

EXHIBIT 3

MOTIVATION AND MAINTENANCE NEEDS COMPARED

	MOTIVATION NEEDS	MAINTENANCE NEEDS
ORIGIN	Human tendency of becoming	Animal tendency of survival
CHARACTERISTICS	More psychological in nature Long duration of satisfaction Satisfaction/no satisfaction Goal-oriented	More physical in nature Short duration Dissatisfaction/no dissatisfaction Task-oriented

SOURCES OF SATISFACTION AND DISSATISFACTION	Job content,
	   mainly internal to the person
	Work itself
	Personal standards
		Job context,
		   mainly external to the person
		Work environment
		Impersonal standards

MANIFESTED NEEDS	Achievement Growth Responsibility Recognition	Physical Social Status Orientation Security Economic

[3] M. Scott Myers, "Who Are Your Motivated Workers?" *Harvard Business Review*, January–February 1964.

[4] A. H. Maslow. *Motivation and Personality*, Harper & Brothers, 1954.

In the business organization, *job content* is the source of motivation while *job context* is the source of maintenance (Exhibit 3). Thus group-administered benefits, automatic raises, working conditions, and job security are ways to serve employees' maintenance needs but do not produce motivated workers. Nor do work goals imposed upon employees motivate them unless there is involvement in goal setting, regardless of how well management's objectives are communicated. Maintenance factors, however, can be sources of tremendous dissatisfaction, particularly if motivation needs are blocked.

Motivation needs are the factors that can produce effective job performance because most of them are satisfied through work itself. Once an individual has committed himself to organizational objectives, his potential is tremendous—provided his own goals and those of the company have been allowed to influence each other. Further, when a man is highly motivated, maintenance needs have less effect on his performance.

Motivation-seeking individuals go to great lengths to reach personal goals, with relatively little concern for maintenance needs. For example, plant workers may ignore a degree of dissatisfaction with physical conditions or security as long as their sense of achievement is high. Conversely, maintenance-seeking people are never really satisfied; they only temporarily reach a level of no dissatisfaction. That is, if life and work are not satisfying, they will find a host of things to complain about. But taking care of the complaints brings no satisfaction; it just means no complaints on that particular point.

The tragedy of employees at work is that so many try to satisfy their motivation needs through maintenance seeking. Management too has erred in responding to its employees' search for personal meaning and motivation in work with more concern for maintenance instead of motivation needs.

Chapter 5

Goal-Oriented People

M OTIVATION SEEKING HAS BEEN DESCRIBED, ALSO, AS GOAL-ORIENTED OR GOAL-seeking behavior, and the research on achievement motivation identifies much the same characteristics.* Managers can therefore operate on the principle that motivated people are those who are goal-oriented. To repeat: The goals they seek will be personal, but under the right conditions the achievement of these personal goals will result in the achievement of company objectives.

The process that facilitates this interaction has been briefly described as goal setting. Whether individual and organizational goals are identical is secondary to this process. The primary consideration is whether the resulting action will help achieve both goals. The very way in which goal-oriented people go about seeking personal fulfillment will achieve business targets as well—if these goal-oriented people can perceive a relation between what they want to do and what someone else wants to do.

Some people are task-oriented rather than goal-oriented (Exhibit 4). They have learned from experience—possibly through parents or supervisors —not to seek goals but simply to perform tasks without regard for the results. Their behavior omits a standard of performance. The implications for supervision are obvious; many of these people can be taught to be goal seekers—and it is clear that for an organization to achieve its objectives it must be staffed with people who are demonstrably goal-oriented.

---

* David C. McClelland, *The Achieving Society*, D. Van Nostrand Company, 1961.

EXHIBIT 4

TENDENCIES OF THE GOAL-ORIENTED VS. THE TASK-ORIENTED PERSON

GOAL-ORIENTED INDIVIDUAL	TASK-ORIENTED INDIVIDUAL
1. Seeks feedback and knowledge of results. Wants evaluation of own performance. Wants concrete feedback.	1. Avoids feedback and evaluation. Seeks approval rather than performance evaluation.
2. Considers money a standard of achievement rather than an incentive to work harder.	2. Is directly influenced in job performance by money incentives. Work varies accordingly.
3. Seeks personal responsibility for work if goal achievement is possible.	3. Avoids personal responsibility regardless of opportunities for success.
4. Performs best on jobs that can be improved. Prefers opportunity for creativity.	4. Prefers routine nonimprovable jobs. Obtains no satisfaction from creativity.
5. Seeks goals with moderate risks.	5. Seeks goals with either very low or very high risks.
6. Obtains achievement satisfaction from solving difficult problems.	6. Obtains satisfaction not from problem solving so much as from finishing a task.
7. Has high drive and physical energy directed toward goals.	7. May or may not have high drive. Energies are not goal-directed.
8. Initiates actions. Perceives suggestions as interference.	8. Follows others' directions. Receptive to suggestions.
9. Adjusts level of aspiration to realities of success and failure.	9. Maintains high or low level of aspiration regardless of success or failure.

Who Are the Goal Seekers?

Extensive research shows consistent patterns in the work lives of so-called goal seekers. These people exhibit confidence; they are action-minded and expect to win. In fact, they habitually select activities where they have a chance of winning. They also have a tendency to make career, education, and work decisions without seeking help or advice (hence the dislike of close supervision). They feel a strong need to tackle tough goals and achieve them, not just well but with excellence. They set long- and short-range goals for themselves and plan their lives ahead. They don't describe themselves as lucky; instead, they believe they make their own luck.

The goal-oriented person seeks feedback and knowledge of results. He constantly puts himself in the position of being evaluated not only by his supervisor but, more importantly, by himself and by the evident results of his work. He wants this feedback to be individualized; that is, he wants his own performance and not that of the group evaluated. Does this mean that goal seekers may be independent of company values and goals? In a sense the answer must be "yes," but the goal seeker who works for a large corporation is bound to see that one route to his personal goals is through the achievement of company objectives and to cooperate accordingly.

In contrast, the task-oriented person is concerned just with doing his job, not with the end results. He is likely to avoid feedback and evaluation. Rather, he seeks approval.

If a plant visitor were to stop alongside an assembly line and ask the workers, "What are you making?" the goal-oriented employee might describe the end product. The task-oriented person, on the other hand, would more likely say, "$2.35 an hour." The point here is that the motivated man sees himself as an individual contributor to company objectives, while the task-oriented worker wants only to be a part of the group and take on the protective coloring of his environment.

The goal seeker, because of his sense of individual responsibility and concern for ends rather than means, may be viewed by supervisors as disruptive to the work flow. And he may very well be a problem because he tends constantly to ask, not what is being done, but why it is being done. Whenever work progress is being reported, a project is being organized, or he is participating in a management committee meeting or a problem-solving conference, he will have three favorite questions: "What do you mean?" "How do you know?" and, "As compared to what?"

What About Money?

What is the effect of pay upon the behavior of the goal-oriented as compared to the task-oriented employee or manager? To the goal seeker money is a standard of achievement rather than an incentive to work harder. This must not be interpreted to mean that the goal seeker is indifferent to salary, raises, or discretionary financial rewards; it's simply that he uses money as a way of knowing how well he is doing in relation both to his personal goals and to company objectives. In other words, it is one form—and a very important one—of the feedback to which he looks for a reflection of his individual effectiveness. If he feels that the money he receives for his work does not reflect his contribution properly, he will be dissatisfied.

The goal seeker is particularly susceptible to dissatisfaction with money that comes to him simply as a result of his membership in the group. Therefore, salary administration plans which are based on automatic increases, formulas, or group incentives are not effective motivators as far as he is concerned. Merit pay is, according to industrial research, the better company policy.

Now let's consider the task-oriented employee. His job performance is directly influenced by money incentives, and it varies accordingly. His productivity increases if a carrot is dangled before him, as does his aggressiveness in furthering company objectives. This is not to say that companies cannot get effective performance by financial incentives—obviously they can. However, it does mean that the motivated person—that is, the one who is most likely to contribute to company goals—is interested in achievement itself for personal reasons, although it should hardly be necessary to add that if you stop paying him, or if management fails to reward him for setting a target and meeting it, then he will go elsewhere.

What about the company which has an incentive plan that apparently is working well? Should management abandon it simply because motivated people are less likely to respond to this form of compensation than to others? Of course not—any firm that did so might be making a fatal error. If salesmen, for instance, are being paid on an incentive basis and the plan seems to be working, there is no good reason for changing it, even though its effectiveness may indicate that the salesmen are task- rather than goal-oriented (a change in the method of compensation might leave them confused and unproductive). The trouble with incentive plans is that salesmen, like clever lawyers, can always find a way of beating the system; the group very often becomes a chief factor in thwarting management's attempts to manipulate individual behavior through incentives, piece rates, and other compensation policies geared to units of output.

The important thing for management to understand is that for the goal-seeking person financial incentives are not enough. Besides money he wants the personal satisfaction which he sees resulting from the achievement of company goals. Can it sometimes happen that he will be more concerned with personal than with company goals? The answer again is "yes." If, financially and otherwise, management appears to reward conformity to organizational procedures and values more than it does end results, the goal seeker will attempt to do things his own way, or he will leave for a more congenial climate. And the company will in all probability be the loser.

Attitudes Toward Responsibility

Many performance appraisal and review programs are concerned with acceptance of responsibility and accountability. Job descriptions have among their objectives the identification of performance standards. What effect does this emphasis have upon employees?

Supervisors are aware, naturally, that some people will not tackle a job unless they have a chance of succeeding; this, we have said, is a characteristic of goal seekers. But what is to be done about the man who always wants to win and who evades jobs that have little chance of success? Rather than see this type of person as a liability to the organization, management must recognize that along with his habitual addiction to the challenge that is achievable the goal-oriented employee or manager will also seek personal responsibility for the work.

The task-oriented person, on the other hand, avoids personal responsibility regardless of the opportunities for success. Whether in a winning or a losing situation, he does not want to be responsible for the outcome. This is one of the reasons he would rather blend in with the group than stand out. It also supports the idea that he avoids feedback and evaluation and, therefore, will show a definite preference for routine and nonimprovable jobs. In other words, he gets no satisfaction from creativity and innovation but likes jobs that are well defined and orderly and have a management-prescribed way of doing them. The task-oriented person may ask to see his job description or encourage his supervisor to write one for him if none exists. Why? Because, if his job has been determined for him by someone else, he won't have to take responsibility for what happens. His attitude is, "Don't ask me why we do it that way; I just work here."

If management rewards people who do jobs as they are told, the task-oriented person may move upward in the hierarchy. His progress will not be due to any personal abilities he may have; it will mean that following orders pays off. Furthermore, if you suddenly give this man an opportunity to organize his work for himself, to be creative, to think broadly, to consider the relationship of his work to that of others, and to determine the way in which he will support company goals, he probably won't respond for a time. But, if you place a high enough value on this employee's services and organize his work in sufficient detail, then he may be a meaningful contributor to the company's objectives. In short, a task-oriented employee is not invariably undesirable. The company will, however, get precisely the employee behavior the work environment rewards.

The goal seeker, on the other hand, is always trying to change the way things are done. If management is unable or unwilling to adjust to change, it should not hire goal-oriented people. The question is, what are the opportunities for creativity? If we take a goal-oriented and a task-oriented employee and give them the same assignment, the task seeker will probably look at it as just another job, whereas the goal seeker will find opportunities for creativity even in work that has been reduced to mere routine. He will struggle to improve his job even though management has been working very hard to remove every chance for a man to be an individual and reach personal goals.

Risk Evaluation

We have been talking about winning. How do these two very different types of people evaluate risk? Interestingly, research in achievement motivation indicates that the person who prefers goals with either a very low or a very high risk is not actually motivated; a man who wants a job in which he has virtually a 100 percent chance of success is not a motivation seeker. This is not surprising in the light of common sense, but what may be less apparent to many managers is that a person who seeks very high risk situations is in fact neither goal-oriented nor highly motivated.

If we look at the psychology involved, we will see that selecting an objective that has a high risk of failure and little chance of being achieved is a way for a person to avoid personal responsibility. And the task seeker, we remember, shuns feedback, evaluation, and personal responsibility and prefers routine jobs. One obvious way of playing it safe is to tackle the impossible situation, for who can blame someone who aims very high and fails to hit his target? Certainly not the person himself. Thus the compulsive gambler is a perfect example of the task-oriented man. He invariably goes all-out for the "sure thing" or the "long shot." If he loses, it's "the breaks of the game"; in other words, "I'm not the one that fails, it's luck." It is the difference between being "other-directed" and "inner-directed."

We often hear executives bemoaning the scarcity of people with guts and willingness to take risks. If they mean that they want more people who will take very high risks, they are mistaken. However, if what they want is more people who will evaluate the probabilities and risks present in a business situation and then select the strategy which offers a challenge but has a chance of success, that is a concept consistent with the research findings on achievement motivation.

The goal seeker prefers work that involves a *moderate* risk. What is a "moderate" risk as compared to a "high" one? We could turn to statistical decision-making theory as a basis for answering this question; but, in the final analysis, the difference between a moderate risk and a high risk is the perception of the individual making the judgment. What is a high risk to the task seeker may very well be perceived as a moderate risk by the goal seeker. It is a matter not so much of "reality" as of motivation.

Managers should note that when they make up their minds about risks it is important to consider the judgment of the person who will be personally responsible. This is consistent with the results-oriented philosophy of management. A company which is concerned with objectives is more likely to permit an individual to make his own decisions about risks, whereas one which practices management by controls will seek to manipulate the individual's behavior, including his personal motivation and judgment. Above all, the supervisor interested in encouraging employee motivation must not remove all the opportunity for winning or losing from the work of people who are goal-oriented. Decreasing the risk of failure in a job will frustrate the motivated person, however comfortable it may be to the task-oriented employee. This is what happens in the bureaucratic organization: Management removes all opportunities for failure (and individuality); there is a policy for every conceivable situation, and failure is followed by additional policies to take care of the same contingency should it arise again.

Approach to Problems

This brings us to the next characteristic that discriminates between the two types of people. The goal seeker gets much satisfaction from solving difficult problems, whereas the task seeker gets satisfaction not so much from problem solving as from finishing a task. In a word, the task-oriented person's objective is to get through. Not to get through with excellence but simply to get the work out. This follows from his tendency to avoid feedback, evaluation, and personal responsibility and his preference for routine jobs. He sees problems as problems and not as challenges. Because he also sees them as threats to his security, being faced with one may make him feel insecure, inadequate, anxious. To spare himself, therefore, his approach is to get the job over and done with and avoid problems and improvements. The goal seeker, however, *likes* problems—difficult ones that carry with them a moderate risk but give him chances to prove himself and obtain feedback on his performance.

We are often impressed by displays of energy. We tend to seek and hire people who have high drive and lots of physical expressiveness. These qualities may be found among both goal-oriented and task-oriented employees; however, their presence or absence is not so important as the fact that they are properly directed. It is not unusual to find a person who has lots of energy but seems to get nothing accomplished. Physical energy is necessary but not sufficient for problem solving and the achievement of goals; obviously, if a man does not have it, he will be unable to sustain his activities— which makes it a prerequisite for job success in any case. What we should be concerned with is whether or not he does anything with it and whether or not it is in gear with his work.

The task-oriented employee is more likely to be a follower than a leader, receptive to suggestions and easy to get along with (except when frustrated in finishing a task). Consequently, he is often well liked, and his willingness to cooperate is seen as a desirable characteristic. It does, in fact, simplify a supervisor's role; but, looked at from another point of view, it is an indicator of low motivation. Motivated people initiate action, and while they may follow leaders they respect, they prefer to be their own leaders. Close supervision is something they can do without.

The goal seeker with a difficult problem to solve regards suggestions as interference. This may at times cause supervisors to call him "willful" and "independent," which are not necessarily inappropriate labels. He also is concerned with improving his job, so that he may resist suggestions in this area too; in fact, if he is strongly motivated, he may even attempt to prove that the supervisor's suggestions are wrong. Does this mean that he is obstinate or stubborn? Under continuing close supervision it may, because the philosophy of management by controls is entirely foreign to his personality.

Will the strongly motivated person come into occasional conflict with other people? Yes. Whether this is good or bad, however, depends upon the company's values. If it places a high value upon docile followers who respond well to suggestions and like to be told how to do their jobs, then it is no place for the goal-oriented manager or employee. If we are to enjoy the benefits of the motivated person who thinks and acts as an individual, then we must allow him latitude to express his individuality. Seldom, though, will he think of resistance to suggestions and conflicts with other people as directed toward personalities; such considerations have little meaning for him (conversely, the task-oriented person may be obsessed with personalities). If this is disturbing to management, it may be a sign that management itself is in error rather than the individual.

Level of Aspiration

In our American culture we have considerable folklore about setting our sights high. Graduation speeches and inspirational pleas from management speak of the glories of boundless aspiration. They may have a stimulating effect, but for part of their audience they are superfluous. Some people maintain a high level of aspiration regardless of the success or failure that they actually experience in life.

We have already described the task-oriented person as seeking goals with either very high or very low risks much as the gambler does. Now we also find him keeping his level of aspiration consistently high or consistently low. Take the man who aims low. Regardless of how many successes he may have, he never raises his sights because, from his viewpoint, doing so might invite failure. It is not likely that management will place a high value upon such an employee; however, it may be fooled into placing a lot of faith and hope in his counterpart whose level of aspiration is high. Yet, if the optimist's hopes for the future remain high even when experience should have taught him that they are unrealistic, here again we have a task-oriented person. He does not respond to true feedback because he avoids evaluation, and he never integrates successes and failures into his motivation pattern.

We should not admire the person who persists in an activity when he has had failure after failure. Rather, we should understand that his behavior is not in keeping with the realities—in contrast to the goal seeker who continually adjusts his level of aspiration.

When the goal seeker wins, he aims a little higher the next time; when he loses, he aims a little lower. If he reaches a difficult goal, his next objective will be even more difficult; but, if he loses, he will choose a more moderate risk. Because he is compulsively and habitually seeking to win, he uses feedback to modify his ambitions in accordance with the facts. This means that he will win more often because he has learned to make fine discriminations among strategies.

Not Discrete Categories

We have been painting a very black and very white picture of the goal seeker and the task seeker. So perhaps it should be pointed out that these are not discrete categories but are actually a continuum.

The advantage of describing the extremes of this continuum is that it allows us to focus sharply upon differences in motivational patterns. We find people with all degrees of motivation, and we find individuals who move in one direction or the other during their lifetimes. We also find concentrations of the one or the other type within companies, depending upon the nature of the corporate environment.

If we understand these behavior patterns in their purest and most extreme forms (as they are described here), then as managers we should be able to recognize them when we see them demonstrated by real-life people. We should also have some idea how the company climate can affect behavior. We should, in fact, be asking some questions: How can one turn a task seeker into a goal seeker? Is it possible to change a person in so basic a way, even though tendencies toward either orientation are thought to develop early in life and to be strongly influenced by parents' child-rearing practices? How does one tell a goal seeker from a task seeker, inside the company or out? What are the company conditions that encourage the one or the other behavior?

This last question is the key to the matter. We need to look at the company itself, for even the best-motivated person cannot long survive in a company that is essentially task-oriented.

The Goal- Versus the Task-Oriented Company

Because the organization is a collection of people, generally similar in background, it is the manifestation of its members' personalities, especially that of the chief executive. The organization itself is sometimes said to have "personality." By analogy, then, we can speak of being either goal- or task-oriented. And—to carry the analogy still further—if we look at what is said orally and in print on behalf of the company; if we examine its decisions and plans, its values and beliefs, its purposes and above all its folklore, myths, and corporate heroes, then we can get some clues to its motivation.

We have already talked about purpose. The company that does not identify its purpose—that is, its reason for existence—denies its people a significant opportunity to add meaning to their work lives. We have said, too, that profit is an incentive, not a goal in and of itself, and the organization's purpose should therefore be described as something else—generally, to serve some particular need of society as well as its members' own needs. What we require, therefore, is a standard, a way of measuring how well these needs are being met. And, in a free enterprise system, our standard is money.

There is nothing un-American about making money; for that matter, it is quite American and consistent with the spirit and principles of free enterprise. The real question is what money means to the business.

Suppose we have two drug firms, both dealing in ethical pharmaceutical products. Perhaps one keeps only the highly profitable products in its line, dropping those that bring in less than an acceptable return without regard to the needs of physicians, their patients, and society. We make no attempt here to judge whether this is proper conduct on the part of the company; we simply say it has made profit its No. 1 goal.

But let's suppose that the other drug firm carries in its line products which lose money as well as products which make money. How does that company define its purpose? Obviously its goal cannot be simply to make a profit; if that were so, the losing products would be eliminated. Is this second firm goal-oriented, and should the first then be called task-oriented?

The hypothesis which we offer here is that the company which is directly influenced by money incentives (look at the president—how does he react?) and varies its activities accordingly can be termed task-oriented. However, the one which uses money as a standard of achievement rather than its prime goal can be characterized as goal-oriented. The difference is one of basic motivation.

This is, in fact, a plea for the free enterprise system. Just as the goal-seeking person is a product and a producer of the free enterprise system, the goal-oriented company is more consistent with the concept of free enterprise than the task-oriented company. We might even say that an organization which has as virtually its only objective the making of money is out of place in that system. It is not a question of ethics but, again, a question of motivation, particularly the motivation of the chief executive. If he personally responds mainly to financial incentives, it is likely that the other members of the organization will behave in the same way. Taken as a group, they will avoid feedback and evaluation, avoid personal responsibility, lack creativity, and seek goals with very high or very low risks.

The success of free enterprise does not depend on companies which have aimed at low-level goals. The American business system was built by people who sought reasonable risks; it cannot tolerate companies which seek only low risks. And it cannot tolerate those which seek only high risks. In fact, high-risk business ventures should logically be more characteristic of socialized or communistic societies, because if the government owns most of the resources, investment capital and productivity do not become personal responsibilities.

Creativity, too, is characteristic of the goal-oriented rather than the task-oriented company. People prefer challenge and improvement. They derive constant satisfaction from solving difficult problems. They exercise initiative. They view controls as interference. And what better description is there of the free enterprise system, and what better resistance to communism, than company presidents and employees at all levels who resent controls, whether governmental or supervisory?

Mature Company—Mature Employees

Some presidents of great corporations make a great deal of noise about the socialism that is creeping into the "American way of life," while at the same time they operate private socialistic systems within their corporations. This attitude is an expression of Theory X at the corporate level, as, incidentally, socialism and communism are the practice of Theory X at the national and international levels. Health insurance, job security, and pensions are excellent maintenance factors; without them, people would be dissatisfied. But before we conclude that it is good or bad at the national level, the corporate level, or even the individual, private level to have such benefits, either publicly or privately administered, let us state that it is irrelevant. What *is* relevant is how they came into being. A company which says, "We know exactly what type of hospital room is best for our employees," is guilty of just as much socialism as a state or federal government which claims the same superior knowledge—and at the state and federal level there is at least a measure of individual decision and responsibility through the processes of democracy. Similarly, union members have a right to seek more benefits (or to put pressure on management for more benefits), although this is not motivation but, rather, maintenance seeking.

What organizations might do when they institute insurance programs and other benefits would be to determine how much money should be spent on them, establish objectives for them, and then permit and encourage the employees to decide how the money should be spent and how much of their own money should be deducted from their pay to augment benefits. True, an equivalent could be given in direct salary, and the individual might be left to make his own decisions about his needs; however, it is of course unrealistic to think that a trend of many years could actually be reversed or attenuated. Besides, group buying has a price advantage. None of this is, of course, a substitute for management planning, coordination, and perspective; but why couldn't a company involve its employees in determining how the insurance program, for instance, should be structured? Then they would feel a personal responsibility toward it, and benefits could become more of a motivator and less of a dissatisfier.

To allow this type of involvement is highly consistent with the goal approach. A company that is interested in increasing the number of goal seekers among its employees should increase the opportunities for personal responsibility. And what greater responsibility in the field of benefits than making your own decisions? The goal-seeking individual does not want a father image at work. Benevolence and paternalism lead to childish behavior; for example, companies have experienced great employee unrest immediately after granting an additional holiday or an improved retirement program in the manner of the good father looking after his children. Therefore, the mature organization deals with employees in a more mature and individually responsible way.

Competition with Standards

What are your company's myths, and who are its heroes? Does it believe that "nice guys finish last"? If so, it may encourage more concern for competitiveness with colleagues than for the achievement of mutually acceptable objectives.

Again we know from research that the achievement-oriented person does to a degree use his peers as a base for measuring his own success. However, he is more likely to use personal standards of his own which he has developed as a result of past competition. This does not mean that competition among organizations or among individuals is not good; rather, it should tell us that a singular belief that success is to be judged in relation to others instead of one's personal standards is less than satisfactory.

The goal-oriented company competes with its own standards of achievement more than with its competitors. Its goals and plans are its own, not the reflection of another firm's long-range planning. If the company sets its objectives in terms of matching or surpassing a competitor's growth, then it is just as much a follower as the task seeker. The goal-oriented company sees the performance of other firms as an index of how well it is doing but not something to be imitated.

Finally, are the corporate heroes people who work long and hard or are they the ones who simply get the job done? Do they conform, or are they individuals? Is there more reward for people who set the limits or for people who push the limits of acceptable corporate practices? Which speaks with greater authority—the policy manual or the voice of the individual results-oriented manager? These are the signs by which we distinguish the goal-seeking company from the task-seeking crowd.

Chapter 6

Increasing Goal-Oriented Action

IMPROVEMENT BEGINS AT THE TOP. SUPERVISORS WHO WANT PEOPLE TO BE CON-cerned about goals and goal achievement must practice what they preach. That is, they must do what they encourage their employees to do.

If the organizational climate is not conducive to achievement motivation, then we should not expect employees to be goal-minded. What do we mean by "climate"? One important element in it is management—including first-line supervisors. If they themselves are low on achievement motivation, then it would be unreasonable to expect nonsupervisory employees to seek opportunities for goal fulfillment.

Other factors, such as company policy and practice and the procedures for recognizing outstanding achievement, influence managerial and nonmanagerial personnel alike. In fact, they must influence managers and, above all, supervisors as much as or more than any other group in the organization. For in simple terms, as far as employees are concerned, managers and supervisors *make* the company environment.

Achievement Motivation and Organization Structure

What are some of our assumptions about achievement motivation? First of all, it is an individual characteristic. It cannot be institutionalized; that is, we cannot get greater levels of achievement by adding more "organization."

Research in industrial psychology has shown that the motivated organization will have low "structure"; in other words, it will follow what has been termed "free form" management. Communication is important to it—and a vital part of communication is written policies, written procedures, and organization charts. True absence or neglect of these would produce institutional chaos or at least a low level of receptiveness; therefore, the motivated organization seeks to use them properly—avoiding, however, the rigid conformity which has a straitjacketing effect. An institution in all its complexities cannot be put in writing completely, and any attempt to do so and then to adhere strictly to the words and lines committed to paper destroys flexibility. Suffice it to say that there is often great discrepancy between the policy manual and what is actually going on.

Low structure should not, however, be thought of as peculiar to either formal or informal organization. It means that, in reality, the organization is determined by the corporate objectives—by the nature of the jobs to be done, the people by whom and with whom they are to be done, and the way in which one activity ties in with another. And experience tells us that the results often bear little resemblance to the formal organization chart itself.

Low structure can also be thought of as implying freedom to act on one's own and to initiate contacts with anyone in the organization who may be necessary to get the work done—without regard to protocol and without going up the organizational ladder so as to branch over to another chain of command. Instead, individuals go wherever they need to in achieving their objectives. Thus low structure makes possible the sort of informality which is expressed by close personal relationships and few status differentials. Basically, individuals deal with individuals, not with impersonal authority and rules. Many companies may *think* they have low structure, with a friendly, free-form type of management and the opportunity to seek information and assistance as needed, but unless their people actually feel and believe that this is so, it will not show up in their work behavior.

The low-structure organization, in short, shifts constantly. It organizes itself around objectives rather than elaborate official charts, reporting relationships, and job descriptions which specify formal channels of communication and strict measures of accountability. Most important of all, its members are free—and know they are free—to function as their jobs require.

Opportunity for Responsible Behavior

Another characteristic of the achievement-motivated organization is a high concern for responsibility. This has nothing to do with the responsibilities which are defined by a man's job description and are imposed upon him with the implied threat of punishment if he doesn't live up to them. Responsible organizational behavior comes from a personal commitment to company objectives as well as one's own personal goals and not from detailed lists of job assignments.

Concern for responsibility must be manifest in the behavior of managers and supervisors. It is encouraged and developed, not by what management says or causes to be written in job descriptions or company pronouncements, but through action and example. It is not, in other words, a proper subject for statements of policy.

Goal seekers will evidence a sense of personal responsibility as a basic function of their motivation pattern. It can be developed among other employees by giving them an opportunity to assume responsibility. Very often managers deplore the rank and file's lack of commitment to company objectives and the lack of adequate follow-through in getting a job completed when, in fact, they have designed the job in such a way and have oversupervised it to such an extent that there is no room left for the individual to be responsible. He doesn't have to be—someone else is responsible for him.

Creating the opportunity for responsibility, in the sense of responsible mature job behavior, goes far beyond saying to a person, "I am going to hold you responsible for the completion of this task." That is only a part of it. Responsibility cannot survive when a supervisor hovers over his employees, giving the impression that they either are stupid or are otherwise not to be trusted. What it comes down to is being responsible for our own behavior. And, in order to learn this, we must have the opportunity as persons to be individual contributors not only to company goals but to our own futures.

The Fear of Punishment

Remembering, too, that goal seekers do not like conditions of either zero risk or excessively high risk, we must be sure not to offer people only opportunities for "sure things" or charge them with impossible tasks. Otherwise, we are setting up demotivating situations.

The degree to which one will be rewarded for success or punished for failure defines risk. But does punishment have a place in the industrial organization? Will it prevent behavior which does not contribute to company goals? Discharge is a punishment, but keeping an employee in the company when he cannot afford to quit and there is no possible opportunity for him to make any real contribution is a worse one. It bears a strong analogy to "brainwashing," which may have been invented not by the Communists but by management.

Certainly we can find many companies which are perpetuating ideal conditions for brainwashing. That is, they are punishing the individual for being himself and holding certain values, and at the same time they are rewarding him for changing his values—all this within an environment of threat and anxiety, the threat of imminent disaster, and enforced conformity to rules and subordination to others. What is right one day is wrong the next; what top management says contradicts what the immediate supervisor says; and rewards and punishments appear to be doled out capriciously, with no relation to identifiable achievement. At the very least, this sort of inconsistency produces an atmosphere of conformity, lethargy, and maintenance-seeking behavior; psychologically speaking, it is one of the most destroying experiences a person can undergo.

Psychology tells us, moreover, that punishment serves only as a deterrent. In other words, it teaches us what not to do, but it fails to teach us what we *should* do, and it works only so long as the threat of punishment is present. It may lead to gamesmanship in which people are motivated only to challenge authority by doing the forbidden thing. And, with the sensitive employee already conscious of failure, it may be totally unnecessary; the blundering supervisor, himself immature, may merely add insult to injury. (How many supervisors who treat their children like adults still treat their subordinates in plant or office like children?)

In answer to our original question, then, the idea of punishment is inconsistent with the idea of individual responsibility. It may have its place, but so far as the business organization is concerned it is some other place.

The Positive Reward

Rewards can be equally misunderstood and misapplied. If we use them only to increase conformity, then we must inevitably look to greater and more costly rewards to produce the desired behavior, and it is not likely that the company can go on devising new ones indefinitely.

To go back a little, there are rewards and there are maintenance factors, and the difference between them has to do with the way they are realized. Maintenance factors are group-determined. Rewards by their very nature are individual; while they may originate on a group basis, they ultimately involve a unique personal decision. To be positive, they must be tied to individual contributions to company objectives. Further, they must be understood in terms of the receiver and not the giver. Sometimes, unfortunately, managers reward people as they themselves would like to be rewarded, although it does not follow that rewards have the same meaning to everyone.

Perhaps this is why money is so often used as a reward. It has the advantage, at least in our American culture, of being almost a universal satisfier. Yet money, as we have seen, can also be a source of dissatisfaction, particularly when it bears no relationship to what a person has accomplished but simply comes to him automatically as it does to everyone else, whether he has done just a minimal job or an outstanding job. The goal seeker—who, we know, does not respond to financial incentives in a direct cause-and-effect relationship; who considers money a standard of achievement rather than achievement itself—may place a higher value on opportunity to grow and to achieve personal goals.

For this type of employee the reward which is "given" is less than the one which he gets for himself through his own actions. That is why explaining the merit-pay system to him is likely to produce better results than keeping it a mysterious process in which employees get "handouts" in a way which makes it difficult for them to see what they are being rewarded for.

Interpersonal Relations

Interaction among individuals, particularly supervisory and nonsupervisory employees, constitutes another critical element of the organizational climate. A supporting environment is not one in which the organization administers to every individual's needs on a *carte blanche* basis. Rather, it is simply one in which the attitude prevails that "I, the supervisor, recognize you as an individual person and I deal with you as such."

Positive interpersonal relations leave little room for anxiety and threats. True, supervisors sometimes worry about establishing too close relationships with employees and are often counseled to avoid becoming unnecessarily involved. The rationale behind this is the idea that the supervisor manages by virtue of his authority and superior position in the company and that warm supportive interpersonal relations with subordinates may be damaging to his power. The danger may be a real one for the many supervisors who are concerned only with the immediate task and use threats of punishment (or the giving or withholding of rewards) as their main management technique, but any supervisor who can achieve his objectives only by keeping people at a distance and by threatening them has very meager resources.

Authority relationships are the refuge of incompetents—and of supervisors who themselves are threatened by warm personal relationships with others. A person who keeps his subordinates at a psychological distance often has the same type of relationship with his own boss. This simply reinforces the idea that the organizational climate is something whose nature is determined at the top of the organization, starting with the president and penetrating down through the various levels. It supports the notion that, just like top-down planning, top-down motivation depends on practicing what you preach.

A manager who wishes to develop the concept of achievement motivation and personal responsibility among people and expects to see goal-directed behavior as a result, must indicate his concern by his own actions. In fact, a high level of motivation can be a corporate objective in and of itself, no less important than other business goals. Research has established a definite relationship between the level of achievement motivation among people in all echelons of the organization and the company's rate of economic growth.

Motivation, therefore, is no cure-all that managers and supervisors can direct exclusively to nonsupervisory personnel. If management is concerned over lack of motivation and goal-directed behavior among lower-level employees, it must look to itself for the reasons and it must treat itself if it is to effect a cure.

What the Supervisor Can Do

Given these prerequisites, what specifically can be done to increase goal-oriented action? What can top management do for itself and for middle management? What can middle management do for first-line supervision, and what, in turn, can individual supervisors do for individual nonsupervisory employees?

1. *Take responsibility for results and push the limits.* Supervisors who resist accepting the blame for failure to reach goals get the same response from their employees. The healthy, creative organization accepts responsibility for its actions and habitually pushes the limits of acceptable practice. Furthermore, creativity will survive only where policies and precedents are flexible.

As organizations get larger, older, and more complex, staff groups often are set up to write manuals, to codify acceptable behavior and define punishments for going beyond the limits. This may be a sign of organizational "hardening of the arteries." Groups which develop many rules (and even rules about rules), which reward knowing and following the rules just as they punish bending and breaking them, cannot expect motivation-seeking behavior.

There is a pronounced tendency in the business situation as in any group to restrict initiative by forcing conformity to cultural norms. It is virtually impossible for an individual to resist being converted to the attitudes and values held by the majority. In fact, in the typical organization the only way a person can resist group pressure is to leave or be removed from the organization. It is possible, however, for two or more individuals to withstand group pressure indefinitely. Thus, if innovation and creativity are to persist in a work group, supervisors must support "deviant" behavior as long as it is compatible with company goals.

Rather than avoid responsibility for evolving company policy, then, managers and supervisors alike should welcome it. They should continually test its limits and encourage others to do the same thing.

2. *Set challenges and targets.* Goal setting is more likely to occur when work is described in terms of opportunities to set goals—in contrast to work which is defined as tasks to be performed, activities to be continued, and processes to be administered. For example, suppose your boss says, "Your job as marketing manager is to find what customers have needs that can be served by the development and manufacturing capabilities of our company." But what if he were to say this: "Your job as marketing manager is to plan a way to research customer needs, organize a task force, delegate the necessary responsibility, coordinate all the information and reports, and control the ongoing paperwork." Only a task-oriented person needs a job description like the second example to set his specific targets. The goal seeker responds to the first challenge as an opportunity.

The ability of human beings to seek personal and group goals is quite general among the population. It is related to intelligence only insofar as the goals are complex. It is therefore possible for all a company's employees to understand objectives and—more importantly—know how a job should be done to meet them. Supervisors who want to encourage goal-oriented attitudes should therefore think and communicate work assignments in terms of challenges and opportunities to use individual abilities and achieve individual goals while carrying on the company's business.

3. *Expose the employee to competition at his own level.* One of the factors in goal setting is the establishment of standards of performance. Industrial behavioral science research has consistently shown that standards imposed by external authorities tend to be rejected and can be met only by constant incentives and punishments. The same research has shown that competition with others and with self-determined standards is more effective. It does not follow, however, that supervisors should play employees against each other. Competitiveness among team members, if initiated by the leader, often has unfortunate side-effects. Rather, employees should be encouraged to use other people as means of a comparison, to tell how well they are doing.

Standards which are primarily determined by the individual himself are more meaningful to him and are sources of tremendous motivation.

4. *Make feedback and evaluation available.* This will give people an external reference for their progress toward goals as well as the means of achievement.

It has long been traditional in American business for performance appraisals to dwell on personal attributes rather than progress toward goals. However, while these traits may have meaning for character development, they aren't necessarily important to effective work performance. Communicating with employees in terms of the Boy Scout oath (a Scout is loyal, clean, cheerful . . .) may be all very well for a company interested in building friendly relationships among its people, but it is considerably more desirable for feedback to be in terms of work objectives and their achievement.

Performance appraisals in most companies are irrelevant to the job. Supervisors and employees actively ignore the system. In control-oriented firms, higher-level managers use merit rating as a lash to punish or threaten their subordinates, while at the same time they verbalize the virtues of "letting a man know where he stands." Why this failure? One reason may be that performance appraisal systems too often are inventions of the personnel manager. That is, mainstream management has had no part in them.

*Re*viewing performance and *pre*viewing personal targets can serve the purpose of integrating individual and organizational goals only to the extent that

a. The content of the review correlates with company objectives and
b. The process used for evaluating personal performance interacts with the company planning system.

5. *Urge people to increase their abilities continually.* It is quite clear that the development of technology will produce a fall-out of new and different information which will trickle down in some form to people at the lowest level of the organizational hierarchy. Thus anyone who is not continually increasing his ability to do his job is actually falling behind its requirements. There is no escaping the fact that by failing to learn and to seek new experiences he is being a party to his own obsolescence. This is the "Alice in Wonderland effect" in which one has to run to stay in the same place.

Companies have a duty to encourage every employee's efforts at self-development, to make education and training available so as to facilitate personal growth. It is a matter of more than simply having training programs around—and certainly of more than punishing people who do not participate. Increased know-how must have a tangible relevance to goal attainment; that is, supervisors must assist people by stating work objectives in a way that indicates what new skills will be required of them.

6. *Be sensitive to people and their work environment.* This can be depended on to have a significant impact on organizational effectiveness.*

Insensitive managers fail to perceive people as having personal needs and goals because they do not understand their own needs and goals. They cannot possibly tap the human potentialities of people at work. Using, as they do, restrictions, threats of punishment, and psychological distance to control employee behavior, they cannot help but increase feelings of guilt and hostility toward management which result in interpersonal conflict.

Sensitive supervisors, on the other hand, do not practice amateur psychology but are aware of their own needs and goals and thus recognize those of others. Because they are actively working toward goal fulfillment, they can aid others to do so. At the same time they are able to transcend the immediate work environment and deal with the larger purposes of the organization.

7. *Strive for balance between the long-range goals of the individual and those of the organization.* The values of the one are not usually synonymous with the values of the other. People hold concepts about life and seek goals which are not particularly relevant to, or possibly are in conflict with, the organization's. While people are very likely to reach their personal goals through helping to achieve the company's goals, an individual must remain an individual. This is another way of saying that short-term work-oriented goals must not conflict with long-term aspirations that are private as well as personal.

It should be quite clear, in fact, that the concepts expressed here represent a move toward *more* individuality at work, not less, and a means of achieving greater industrial mental health through the intrinsically therapeutic or preventive potential of work itself.

---

* Chris Argyris, *Interpersonal Competence and Organizational Effectiveness,* Richard D. Irwin, Inc., 1962.

PART TWO

The Goal-Achievement Process

Chapter 7

Conditions for Motivation

Can a company become "self-aware"? Can it achieve its objectives at the same time its individual members achieve their personal goals?

These questions we have already asked. We have looked at some of the conditions necessary for individual goal seeking and motivation in the work situation, and we have looked at the relationship between individual and company achievement. But we have yet to give the whole answer as to how, in fact, management can bring these two together.

Because the organization exists in the individual members of the group, for a company to become self-aware it is necessary for all its managers and employees to be aware of themselves as individuals and of their part in furthering its larger goals. This includes the president and other members of top management.

And in what sense are they to become self-aware? The answer this time is basically a philosophical one because the question is philosophical. We are speaking of awareness of self in the process of becoming; that is, becoming more human and achieving the human purposes of self-realization, maturity, and development to the fullest possible degree. Thus everyone in the company, ultimately, must be able to see himself as part of the greater organization and be able to identify his personal goals in the goals of the company. All this we have seen in previous chapters.

But our question must be answered in more than a philosophical manner. It must be answered in realistic terms that will have meaning to each individual as he seeks to understand himself. It cannot be answered by statements from management. The problem can, however, be approached systematically.

The Prerequisites

The conditions necessary to successful synthesis of personal and company goals can be stated as follows:
- An effective, understandable system for identifying company goals.
- A meaningful, clear system for setting personal goals.
- A system for achieving personal and company goal interaction.

What does all this mean? It means in very simple terms what we have been saying all along in this book: that unless the company can determine where it is going, it will be impossible for its individual members to know where they are going, either for themselves or for the company. It means that personal goal setting cannot work effectively unless the company planning system also works effectively. It means, for instance, that performance review and personal development will have no point unless the company has established its objectives in a way which makes them just as understandable and communicable to its employees as they are to its top executives.

True, company goals may exist. But they may be completely unyielding, cast into concrete which has hardened before they can be communicated. This is unfortunate. Individual goal setting is futile where company plans have been made once and for all and cannot be changed. We cannot ask a person to find his proper place in a company, adjusting his goals to corporate goals, unless we also are willing to consider the possibility that modification of company objectives may on occasion be called for.

Neither extreme—no stated, communicable goals at all or rigid, inflexible goals with no chance of change—is conducive to achievement, whether we are thinking in terms of the individual or the organization. That is why we insist on the importance of goal-setting systems specifically designed to produce involvement.

The Necessary Steps

The obvious first steps have already been suggested. It will do no harm, however, to spell them out in more detail here.

We start, of course, with a statement of purpose, derived from the personal values of the president and other key members of the organization, under which the essentially human purposes of all its members are to a degree achievable. For instance, the corporate purpose might be stated as the intention "to serve society by facilitating the growth of the organization, its members, and its customers" (Exhibit 5).

The company purpose will determine just which needs of its customers, and of society in general, it expects to serve; and these in turn will give rise to the company's own needs. The needs of the customer, that is, can be conceived of as interrelated with those of the company itself. They are basically achievement-oriented, and they also make motivation opportunities possible for a large number of the employees. In fact, the way in which company needs are conceived and stated will be a critical factor in the creation of a climate in which people can satisfy personal needs at the same time and by the same work that company needs are satisfied.

The No. 1 company need is to assure the continuity and growth of the

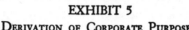

EXHIBIT 5
DERIVATION OF CORPORATE PURPOSE

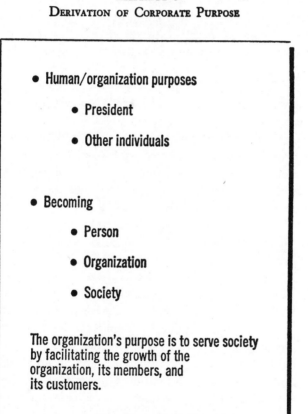

- Human/organization purposes
    - President
    - Other individuals

- Becoming
    - Person
    - Organization
    - Society

The organization's purpose is to serve society by facilitating the growth of the organization, its members, and its customers.

organization. Unless the organization continues in existence (and in the free enterprise system one of the essential ingredients of organizational continuity is growth), there will be no opportunity to satisfy its own needs, the needs of society, or the needs of any of its employees at whatever level. How, then, does a company assure continuity and growth for itself?

All companies—regardless of the type of business they are in—create, make, or market products or services to meet customer needs. The marketing concept today places prime importance upon these needs—and not simply the need of the customer for certain services or certain products, but the need he has to assure the continuity and growth of his own organization. The company that fails to take the needs of the customer into account will soon disappear from the business scene.

In other words, once the company has defined its purpose in whatever terms, it must turn itself to the essential functions within its organization and set these up in a way that will best meet the needs of the same functions within the customer organization. It must identify the customer's objectives and be concerned with them as well as its own. What could be more obvious? Before it can determine what to create, make, or market, it must identify the customer potential for the purchase of that product or service. For the company must maintain a growth trend in earnings per share so as to have the necessary resources to continue to meet customer or company needs and promote continuity and growth. The free enterprise system is built upon this very trend in earnings as measured against capitalization.

Furthermore, we must look to the need for providing opportunity for employees. Here, again, unless the members of the organization can continue to achieve their personal goals, they will not continue to work for it; either they will go and work somewhere else, or they will stay but put forth a bare minimum of effort.

Then there is the company need to be a responsible corporate citizen. What do we mean by this? We are not speaking of social welfare, certainly, or of corporate income tax payments, or even of contributions to local charity. These are simply manifestations of what may or may not be good corporate citizenship. The intent behind them is the main consideration. But, most important, serving as a responsible corporate citizen can be thought of as providing motivation and goal-seeking opportunities for employees and others in the community. Many companies are situated in cities and towns where they are the chief employer and, in fact, are intricately involved with the economic well-being of the community.

The Self-Aware Company

In this situation the self-aware company will understand the influence it has over the lives of many people who do not work for it directly. It will realize that its actions can affect the growth and continuity of the community just as they affect the growth and continuity of the organization and its customers. It will accept the fact that its company responsibility to society at home and at large means, by analogy, that management cannot act in an imperialistic or colonial manner; that is, it cannot be guilty of the sort of conduct that nations have sometimes displayed in exploiting other nations.

A company which establishes a manufacturing facility in a town, uses its labor resources, and so contributes to the economic growth of the community may at the same time send the profits to another part of the country. Perhaps its only reason for moving into the area has been to take advantage of a tax situation; then, through its managers and employees, it begins to demand more community services, more facilities, and ends by complaining about increased local taxes. In its attempt to dominate local politics and influence decisions for its own benefit at the expense of the community, it may virtually eliminate free enterprise for others while it purports to be extending the free enterprise system.

It is not hard to find companies whose managers have a benevolent, paternalistic attitude toward the cities and towns in which they are situated. True enough, in many cases they have saved the economy of a particular part of the nation, but too often it has been at the expense of its people's individuality. These are the managers that are most amazed, after they have saved the destitute community, to find their employees organizing against them.

This kind of corporate behavior epitomizes Theory X in relation to the community. In contrast, serving as a responsible corporate citizen means practicing Theory Y management with respect to the community, whether local, state, or even national, and insofar as possible providing opportunities both for employees and for people who are not the direct responsibility of the firm.

Chapter 8

Motivation Opportunities

THE PROPER IDENTIFICATION OF COMPANY NEEDS, THEN, CREATES OPPORTU-
nities for employees. And making it possible for employees to achieve
personal goals at the same time the company is creating, making, and marketing products or services to meet customer needs provides the necessary
conditions for motivating them to take advantage of those opportunities.
Thus the term "motivation opportunities" as we use it here.

Motivation opportunities may take many forms (Exhibit 6). One of
these, perhaps basic to all the rest, is expansion. If we assure the continuity
and growth of the organization, then we will have expansion and its
derivative—motivational opportunity. Personal growth is necessary to the
individual; corporate growth is necessary to the company. However, since
the main way of achieving personal growth is through work, company
expansion—not to say survival—is critical.

But there are other motivation opportunities.

Decentralization: The Entrepreneurial Organization

Management thinking on centralization versus decentralization has tended
to veer from the one extreme to the other. In the recent past, company
practice has favored decentralization, but the pendulum has lately begun
to move in the opposite direction. Certainly the arguments for and against
each of these two types of organization have been cited many times.

By its very nature, the decentralized company provides more room for personal influence over company goals and therefore more opportunities to set
personal goals. What we are now finding, however, is that we can operate in
a decentralized manner so long as basic objectives are determined by the central management group and then communicated to the decentralized por-

EXHIBIT 6

MOTIVATION OPPORTUNITIES: DERIVATION AND FORMS

COMPANY NEEDS

To assure the continuity and growth of the organization by

- Creating, making, and marketing products or services to meet customer needs

- Maintaining a growth trend in earnings per share

- Providing opportunities for employees to achieve personal goals

- Serving as a responsible corporate citizen

MOTIVATION OPPORTUNITIES

- Expansion

- Decentralization; autonomous, entrepreneurial organization

- Innovation; superior products and services

- Minimal status symbols and informal communication

- High personnel selection and achievement standards

- Independence from third-party intervention

tions of the firm, which in turn add their divisional objectives and devise the strategies needed to reach both corporate and divisional goals. Thus centralization of control and evaluation of goal achievement can be combined with decentralization of decision making and planning.

It is possible, in fact, with a little creativity in organizational planning and structure to obtain the benefits of decentralized organization even within a large corporation that practices centralized, top-down planning and control. The objective in such a creative effort should be to introduce insofar as practical a decentralized form of organization with all it implies, including autonomous divisions. These divisions will be autonomous, that is, in the sense that goal setting is done locally. But it will be done with prior knowledge of overall corporate goals.

It should also be possible to develop within even the largest corporation some of the characteristics of the "entrepreneurial" organization. The word "entrepreneurial" has many connotations; it calls to mind both the small independent businessman and the owner-manager. The concept behind the autonomous entrepreneurial organization is to restore some of the small business atmosphere and character. This can be achieved by the establishment of profit centers, each under the control of a profit center manager who, with his team, is responsible for all the functions needed to create, make, and market their product or service. Opportunities for individual achievement and growth are much more significant under these conditions.

Corporations, however, have in many cases moved away from decentralization because the autonomous divisions or subunits often set and seek goals which do not support corporate objectives. Some people have even concluded that the decentralized organization is intrinsically bad. But nonsupport of corporate objectives should be regarded as basically a symptom rather than a cause. It does not happen because the members of that "small business within the large business" are not interested in serving corporate goals. It most likely happens because they do not know what these objectives are. In other words, corporate planning has not been communicated from the top down, and divisional personnel have not had a chance to become involved in the total goal-setting process.

The point is that centralization must stop short of dictating divisional objectives and strategies which necessarily depend upon a knowledge of local conditions. If *all* goals are established at the corporate level, then we have neither an entrepreneurial organization nor the right conditions for motivation. In fact, we have no incentive for the achievement of corporate objectives. To provide a significant motivational opportunity for divisional management, supervisors, and employees, to combine centralized control effectively with decentralized planning and decision making, corporate goals must be spelled out, then iterated so that we can have both adequate coordination and individual involvement.

Innovation and Excellence

There are more motivational opportunities in the company which invites innovation, which seeks superior products and services, than there are in the one which fails to create, make, and market new products or services or whose objective, stated or implied, it is to be somewhere other than at or near the top in its field. Because the goal seeker, whether he be a manager or a nonmanagement employee, himself seeks excellence and is motivated by conditions in which he can win, it follows that the organization which imitates others will offer an environment less conducive to motivation than that which makes innovation and excellence one of its ways to achieve its goals.

Innovation need not mean simply the creation of new products and services or their manufacture. It can also enter into their marketing. In other words, while a company may follow other corporations in research and development and may use other people's processes for manufacturing, it can still achieve significant growth and continuity by excelling in the marketing arena. Obviously, this is going to be more stimulating to the company's salesmen than to its R&D employees. However, we need to remember that while most of us think of innovation in terms of research and development and engineering, the concept applies equally to many other business functions.

The part of the company that is seldom recognized as offering any innovative possibilities is that which is usually referred to as "staff." Why? Because staff functions are, to most companies, maintenance functions. Staff people often view their role as one of maintaining the mainstream organization and are the last to realize the need for creativity and innovation. They also may be the last to realize the need for superior support of mainstream activities. The idea that a staff group can seek innovation and thereby help the company achieve its objectives is foreign to them. Yet, if there is any part of the organization which is typically in the greatest need of creativity and innovation, it is the staff departments. These frequently are the most demotivated of all.

Management must provide motivation opportunities for these people just as much as for any having to do with the "create, make, and market" functions. This can't be done by *asking* for innovation—the old saying that "necessity is the mother of invention" is quite true. Necessity—that is, need —is an essential first condition. It derives from the company needs that are defined by management. Just like mainstream groups, staff departments can and must have goals defined in these terms, and their goals must be something more than simply "supporting the line organization."

On the other hand, many staff groups set targets and goals for themselves which bear no relationship to the goals of the corporation. Naturally, then, they tend to become autonomous functions. In fact, many apparent staff objectives serve no corporate need and no visible employee need.

For either line or staff groups, innovation therefore is a condition for motivation rather than an end in and of itself. Overall company objectives plus some subobjectives that may involve the organizational subunits in question must be communicated clearly.

Minimal Barriers to Communication

Motivation in terms of personal goal setting and support for company objectives is more likely to occur in organizations that reduce the social and psychological distance between individuals. Barriers to communication and understanding are often set up by the status differences between people—or, more precisely, the differences between people's apparent status. Therefore, management must take positive steps to minimize symbols which serve no purpose except to differentiate between people, and at the same time it must encourage informal communication channels.

The organization chart, for example, may be one of the greatest barriers to communication if it increases the concern that people have for "who can do what to whom." The organization which follows a free-form management style will place little importance upon formal organizational framework and communication patterns, but will build the organization around the goals that must be met.

Position on the company chart of course is indicative of status, but the most prevalent status symbols are the offices of executives and professionals and their furnishings. Minimizing the symbols is not the same thing as eliminating status. Indeed, status cannot be eliminated; it is inherent in the organization because some jobs are more essential to the achievement of goals and some people have more to do than others with the setting of goals.

The kind of status symbols that should be eliminated or reduced in importance are those which stand in people's way, which hinder goal setting and achievement. If we must have these things in order to know who are the key contributors to the organization's goals, then it is obvious that we don't really understand those objectives or other people's role in achieving them.

Many executives and supervisors crave status symbols because they believe these will help them manage better; because, by means of the surroundings and privileges, subordinates will be better able to determine who is in charge. The oversize desk, the paintings, the rug, the draperies, and the secretary who "looks good from the back as well as from the front" all seem to tell everyone, "I am the boss." They are characteristic of the Theory X authority style of management. In fact, believing sincerely that these things stand for responsibility and accountability, nonsupervisory employees will often interpret their own lack of them as reflecting their lack of personal responsibility.

We often assume that the idea of RHIP (Rank Has Its Privileges) is a valid part of management. This concept, however, derives from the precedent set by military organizations and by monarchies, neither of which are altogether the right models for the efficient, effective, goal-seeking business firm. Plush offices, executive dining rooms, parking privileges, expense accounts, club memberships, and potted plants serve only to increase social distance and erect barriers to achievement. If they have this effect, or if people in the company believe that they do, that is simply a sign that all is not well. It is a manifestation of a paranoid tendency within the group. When people are truly important to the company, when they truly support the achievement of company goals, the work itself will be the main status symbol.

The need for status, remember, has been categorized as a maintenance need. The kind of status that might conceivably be useful in a company is the sort which is shared by all its employees. It may be contributed to by the building itself, for instance, or a new and exciting product, or—particularly—the company's reputation in the community and the nation.

Selection and Achievement Standards

High personnel selection and achievement standards provide still another opportunity for motivation. These might, as suggested, include the finding and hiring of people who already exhibit goal-seeking tendencies and have set high personal standards for themselves as evidenced by their past performance. For, unless we hire people who expect as much of themselves as will be expected of them by their supervisors, our chances of motivating the individual (and others in the organization who observe him) will fall far short of creating the environment necessary for growth and achievement.

Also, we must hire for the future as much as for the present. When we consider that a new employee may have 30 or more years with the firm ahead of him, we have to look not just at immediate objectives but at the long-range goals he may well achieve. Contribution over the long term is, after all, the reason for our concern with selection and performance criteria.

If we hire people because we expect a lot of them—and they know this— they will expect even more of themselves. Certainly it is a much greater privilege to be one of these people, to work with them, and perhaps to manage them than to make do with people selected on the basis of low personnel standards.

Independence from Third-Party Intervention

By "third parties" we mean unions, state and federal governments, and any other organizations (for example, trade associations and pressure groups) that may affect the achievement of company and personal goals.

Consider the union. Is it more of an incentive for people within the company to have a union than not to have one? If we will look at the research on achievement motivation, the basis for the motivation-maintenance theory, and the concepts back of Theories X and Y, there is just one conclusion we can reach: that unions can serve only maintenance needs and cannot serve motivation needs. Unions—to repeat—cannot help people set or achieve personal goals; they cannot assist the company in setting or achieving its goals; in fact, they are evidence that motivation opportunities are severely lacking or were lacking sometime in the past.

While motivation opportunities may be quite satisfactory at present, we may still have a union and very little prospect of the members' voting it out. The point has already been made that it takes much better conditions to induce employees to abandon a union than it does to avoid unionization in the first place. Conversely, motivation opportunities must be much worse to get a union than they have to be to keep one. None of this, as we stated earlier, is meant to imply that unions are bad or unnecessary. They are simply made necessary by management.

If satisfaction, happiness, and motivation come from the work itself, then unions are irrelevant to motivation. As a matter of fact, they often operate in a way which results in subdividing jobs and reducing their importance till the workers are mere automatons—interchangeable people making interchangeable parts for interchangeable machines. The presence of a union can also inhibit proper planning and setting of company goals, and it certainly can create conditions that do not encourage the achievement of personal goals. And the time is long past in most companies when attention needed to be focused on such maintenance factors as physical working conditions, job security, fringe benefits, and equitably determined pay.

The unions, however, can serve a very useful purpose in companies which have provided all the maintenance factors but few motivation opportunities. To do this, they must turn their attention to the motivation needs of their members. If management should fail in this area, it may happen that the unions of the future will be the champions of job satisfaction and the achievement of personal goals. Unions and their members are becoming aware of these needs, and if management lags far behind, it may find itself bargaining on motivation.

At the present time, the unions have not awakened to the potential of their members' and future members' motivation needs. In fact, many of their present and past activities are contrary to such an orientation. But, for that matter, so has management's orientation been contrary to its employees' motivational needs. Some companies attempt to prevent the intervention of third parties by granting more and more benefits—vacations, holidays, seniority rights, and the like—and then are quite surprised when people organize and ask for even more. As we know from our research, however, maintenance needs are almost insatiable; that is, whatever we get, we want more. We also know that people are inclined to ask for greater and greater satisfaction of their maintenance needs when we block satisfaction of their motivation needs. The implication for management is that people might be less concerned with security and status needs if their employers were to pay greater attention to motivation needs.

In simple terms, a company should spend as much time, effort, and money improving opportunities for motivation as it does in providing, say, additional holidays and recreational facilities. If our reasoning is correct, then the highly motivated organization in which people are setting and achieving personal goals will experience little or no unrest over maintenance factors.

The future belongs to whichever group is the first to provide significant opportunities for people to satisfy their needs for growth, recognition, responsibility, and achievement. If history has taught us anything, we can predict that should the unions be the leaders, there will be just as much industrial conflict over motivation opportunities as there has been over maintenance factors. And again, if history is any indicator, we can assume that should the unions take the initiative, we will have people seeking personal goals which have been set by a process that did not involve company goals. A time may then come when personal goals are being met through collective bargaining efforts but company goals are not being met at all.

It will be interesting when the first controversy over motivation opportunities reaches the National Labor Relations Board. At any rate, companies that are establishing precedents for providing motivation opportunities and systems under which people can set personal goals that tie in and support company goals will be in a much better bargaining position than those that have ignored psychological needs and actually taken steps to block motivation.

When Is Control Excessive?

A word about government regulation is in order: The economic system in the West requires that a company operate at a profit or disappear. Competition and profit are incentives to provide products and services to meet the needs of customers. The free enterprise system is intrinsically Theory Y in practice, and excessive governmental control is Theory X. But what is "excessive"? What is "intervention"? Protection of patents by federal law is at one extreme, and regulation of profit margins at the other.

Government action is intervention when it takes the "free" out of free enterprise. It is not excessive when firms are prevented from seeking goals that block national objectives by means that are undemocratic. However, "government control" is too often the excuse of incompetent businessmen rather than a statement of the problem. The problem is really barriers to enterprise, profit, creativity and innovation, the pursuit of excellence, and growth.

The answer to the role of government is as complex as the question. Perhaps some clues are to be found in the view that what is intervention by any third party is much akin to task-oriented Theory X management. It is simply different parties blocking growth, achievement, and responsible behavior. The facts of existence and self-awareness apply to the organization and its members alike. External controls never work in the long run. Whether they mean intervention by the government or anyone else, they constitute action which has as its purpose—to borrow from a psychological test for Theory X

attitudes—the preservation of "the American way of life," by force if necessary. This approach has no more chance of succeeding than the establishment of democratic processes by edict—or individual growth under control
by another person.

Chapter 9

Motivation Media

ACHIEVEMENT, GROWTH, RESPONSIBILITY, AND RECOGNITION: THESE BASIC MOTI-
vation needs are imbedded in the essential character of every human
being. In addition to identifying the motivation opportunities that should be
present within the company, management must provide *media* by which the
individual employee can make use of them. It is not enough simply to say
that expansion, decentralization, innovation, adequate provision for informal communication, high personnel standards, and freedom from interference will make it possible for people to satisfy their personal needs and in
turn support customer-company needs. Ways must be provided by which a
person can seek satisfaction through his own actions. Company concepts,
policies, and practices should all be designed to this end.

We have already seen how motivation needs are an individual phenome-
non and how they bear a close relationship to the job. This means that
motivation media must be individually administered (in contrast to group-
administered activities which satisfy maintenance needs). Moreover, if the
purpose of the organization—that is, of all its members from the president
down to the lowest-level clerk or sweeper—is "becoming," then there can be
no inherent conflict between the motivation needs of any two employees, regardless of who they may be. Therefore, motivation media must be available
to essentially everyone on as much of an equal-opportunity basis as possible
rather than being the privilege of a select few. (Notice we say "equal," not
"identical.")

Now let's look at some possible motivation media (Exhibit 7) and see how
they relate to need satisfaction and company achievement.

EXHIBIT 7
POSSIBLE MOTIVATION MEDIA

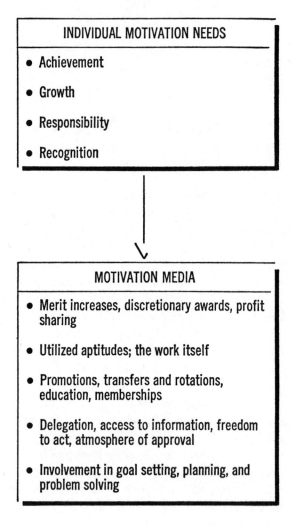

Money as a Motivator

Money is one of the influences that can motivate a person most strongly. The degree to which it does so will depend upon the media used in the determination of wages and salaries. For obvious reasons, merit pay holds the greatest potential. It can take the form of merit increases, discretionary awards, profit sharing, and other such schemes and innovations. All have the advantage of being individually administered and determined by personal contribution to company objectives.

To pay anyone on a merit basis or to give discretionary bonuses and awards, we must of course first know the value of the individual's contribution to company goals. Many pay plans, unfortunately, do not take this into account, the usual reason being the difficulty of determining proper action in individual cases. Yet how acceptable is it to an ambitious, hard-working employee if we tell him we are going to pay him on some automatic basis rather than an individual basis because we don't know how much he is worth to us? Actually, the essential reason behind companies' refusal to consider merit pay is not the problem of having to develop job-evaluation techniques and wage and salary schedules but, rather, failure to set company objectives in a way that will facilitate salary administration.

Incentive plans as we know them today do try to relate compensation to job performance; for example, we often think of the salesman on an incentive plan as getting paid in direct relationship to the value of the orders that he procures. But selling is no longer an entirely individual effort, particularly in the marketing of an industrial-type product. Many other people have been involved in creating and making that product and so have played a part in the successful sale. Just what, then, should the salesman's commission be? Does he deserve all the reward? Combine this line of reasoning with the idea that the truly goal-seeking and achievement-motivated person does not respond to incentives as much as he responds to challenge and we cast serious doubts upon the real effectiveness of incentive schemes. In other words, merit pay is not synonymous with incentives or piece-rate systems, even though, admittedly, these offer individually administered financial rewards for superior performance.

No, the answer lies somewhere in placing a value upon organizational objectives and measuring the contribution that an individual has made to their achievement. Wage and salary surveys which establish pay ranges for whole industries and for types of jobs represent an effort to get at job values, and to a degree these are successful because of the very nature of the competition for skills and abilities. The point, therefore, is not the ability of various schemes to establish merit pay in the best possible way but, rather, the fact that they attempt to do this.

Granted, the difficulties of devising a satisfactory plan of merit pay are very real. There is a temptation to settle for the automatic rate increase that gives everyone an increase because he is a member of the group, whether he barely meets minimum requirements or does an outstanding job. This is one of the areas of personnel administration that needs more attention. If, however, wage and salary administrators will concern themselves with the concept of contribution to company goals, and will back up their concern with sufficient research and innovation, we should be able to devise improved media.

What about discretionary awards? There is a motivating value in, for example, pay increases which come at a time when they are not ordinarily scheduled, just as there is in bonuses, cash awards, and the like. In the last analysis these are matters for judgment, both in their administration and in the development of a medium for implementing them. It is the philosophy behind them, however, that is most critical. If employees understand that they are based purely on merit and contribution to company objectives, and if the way in which management deals with people otherwise has created an atmosphere of trust, they will undoubtedly accept management's judgment.

Profit sharing is probably one of the best motivation media, particularly when it is tied to individual determinants. It is not the fact that profit sharing exists within a company that counts, it is the manner in which it is conceived and expressed to the employees. They must, however, see it as a form of merit pay, not just a benevolent act on the part of management. Profit sharing doesn't come once a year; it is something that goes on constantly within the company on a day-to-day basis. And, if we will provide clearly identifiable ways for people to see that their efforts do contribute to company profit and that they in turn share in this profit, then it can be a great satisfier.

Jobs and Their Design

But the work itself is clearly the most significant medium for satisfying motivation needs. We must turn our attention more closely to the design of jobs. This attention will not be the same sort that has been characteristic, in the past, of industrial engineering efforts to reduce the individual job to the lowest possible level so that any person can do it even though he has few aptitudes and little skill and can easily be replaced. It will take the form of increasing the opportunities for motivation within the job.

Under the concept of job enlargement, instead of subdividing jobs vertically into small discrete tasks we integrate them horizontally within the organization so that a person can see more of the beginning and more of the end of the process which results in the product being offered for sale. This is because part of motivation consists of knowing exactly what you are doing and how it ties into the jobs that precede and follow yours. While lectures and films are useful in communicating this knowledge, they are successful training devices only if the same knowledge is built into the actual work. The increased understanding of company goals which results will in turn encourage the setting of personal goals that support them.

However, the basic aim in job enlargement is to make it possible for people to utilize more of their basic aptitudes, so that they are not expected to perform in a way which dissociates them as individuals from their work. We can hardly approach the man who day in and day out, year after year, simply puts on left-hand door handles and hope to convince him that he is building an automobile. Clearly, he is not using all his aptitudes unless he is extremely limited in intelligence and has a very low level of training.

When a person asks to work for a company, he is asking management to tell him who he is. In other words, work—besides satisfying his needs for achievement, growth, responsibility, and recognition—can help him to be a whole person. For present within everyone is the potential for becoming a healthier, more mature individual, and his job—that important part of his life—must assist him in the search. Automation, incidentally, may be one of the greatest things that ever happened to any industry if only because it takes people away from jobs which are dehumanizing—and there are appalling numbers of such jobs which, far from satisfying human needs for growth, can make people psychologically unhealthy.

Many workers endure jobs that demand little of their true capacity. The challenge of the future is to re-design jobs so that more of this capacity is used, so that they are real motivation media. Then we are much more likely to persuade the employee to support company goals. We can't expect him to be interested in goals when we require him to perform repetitive tasks which have no obvious meaning, nor can we expect him to behave like a human being while his job is robbing him, little by little, of his human characteristics.

Developmental Processes

To be part of an organization which is growing and adjusting to changing conditions is more stimulating than to be associated with one that is shrinking or stagnant. Company growth leads to promotions, to opportunities for meeting new challenges and acquiring new skills.

The motivating properties of "promotion from within" have been recognized by the many companies that have established this as a firm policy. To be sure, what starts out to be a satisfier in some cases turns into a dissatisfier when people are selected for advancement on a straight seniority basis rather than on their ability to make a real contribution. So it is not promotion as such that is motivating but promotion which is an indicator of past achievement and expectations of future achievement. Promotion from within, while good as a general rule, can in fact be demotivating when employees see incompetents achieve high levels in the organization primarily as a function of their length of service. As with all motivation media, consideration of individual abilities and potential is the key factor.

And there are other ways to achieve motivation that also involve a change of job assignment. Transfers and rotations again are a matter of policy and practice with many corporations, but these too are frequently administered across the board without consideration of individual goals or company well-being. Transfers and rotations are simply not things we do without knowing exactly how the new assignment will benefit everyone concerned. Intended to "develop" the individual employee, they sometimes fail to do so because they are undertaken without taking developmental needs into account. Development which is just a corporate version of "musical chairs" is no more than the automatic carrying out of a process without regard for the objectives it is supposed to achieve. Like merit pay and promotion, transfers and rotations are motivating so long as they are handled on an individual basis and not group-administered as a matter of routine.

Then there is continuing education within the corporate framework. Companies often have educational programs and policies regarding membership in professional and business societies—all too many of them, however, with no definite objective in mind. In other words, they administer education as a benefit, not as part of the mainstream of company activity. Yet, if we provide education for employees as we do recreation, because it is supposed in some way to "improve" the employee, we are turning a potential motivator into a maintenance factor.

Many training and education departments exist for themselves alone. They have no clear understanding of how their activities support company goals. In fact, they have a tendency to grow apart from the main organization and become autonomous functions. This condition prevails to such a large extent in American industry that top management might well take a hard look at the resources being spent on education and determine in a specific way what they are getting for their money. Without a clear relationship between education and company objectives we are simply running one more private social welfare system.

However, properly devised education and training programs can be exceptionally motivating. They open a way for the individual to overcome personal barriers that prevent him from achieving his and the company's goals. And not only can extending one's education and acquiring new skills be quite exciting, but it is becoming more and more necessary for employees in all phases of corporate life. They must be encouraged to consider it not a means of preparation for their work but a part of it. In the future, many people will work through several different careers and several completely different occupations during their lifetimes. If education begins only after obsolescence of skills has already developed, we are not only endangering the achievement of company targets but making education a form of punishment for having become useless.

Employees sometimes resist further training because they see no way in which it can help them in their work. When they express this opinion, it is probably because they are quite right. Any number of convincing arguments from supervisors merely aggravates the problem. Training departments must organize their activities in such a way that the relationship between training, either inside the company or out, and the achieving of work goals is self-evident.

Managerial and Supervisory Style

Another set of motivation media relates to managerial and supervisory style. We have already discussed at some length the effects of managers' and supervisors' attitudes and behavior upon employees. Important here are delegation of authority, access to information, freedom to act, and an atmosphere of approval.

A characteristic of the goal seeker, as we now know, is the wish to avoid excessive supervision. Delegation and freedom to act satisfy this need, and the free-form sort of management which does not depend upon formal organizational structure to get things done provides the necessary access to information and atmosphere of approval. All these factors can be summarized as establishing the right conditions for the expression of individuality. They are determined, at least in part, by the supervisor's interpersonal competence.

Involvement and Participation

A miscellaneous group of motivation media includes involvement in goal setting, planning, and problem solving. They will assume many forms and will vary from company to company, but one that is found in increasing numbers of organizations is performance planning and review. It is singled out, not necessarily as an example of the best possible type of involvement and participation, but because it does contain many of the essential characteristics. It will be discussed later in more detail. For the moment let us deal with the more general concepts.

Throughout the preceding chapters we have talked about the proper role of involvement and participation in motivation. Involvement and participation are not motivating in and of themselves except to the extent that they are a means of setting personal and company goals that mutually support each other. "Goal setting" is the general term applied to any procedure within an organization by which we identify those goals and then the methods by which we will achieve them. Involvement in goal setting which management attempts to manipulate in order to give the appearance of individuality but which, in fact, suppresses individuality is not the type we are considering. The goal setting described here is based upon the assumptions of Theory Y and seeks the involvement of employees not because management thinks it will make them happier but because management truly believes that individuals anywhere in the organization will be willing to work toward company goals if they can at the same time achieve some of their personal goals.

It is not even a question whether management likes or dislikes its employees. What is important is, rather, the concept that it respects those employees for the potential contribution to company objectives that they can make if permitted and encouraged to do so. Motivation media, in brief, are the ways in which management expresses its belief in its fellow employees.

PART THREE

Goal-Setting Systems

Chapter 10

A Systems Approach
To Motivation

INDIVIDUAL BEHAVIOR AND ORGANIZATIONAL BEHAVIOR AFFECT ONE ANOTHER IN
ways that cannot be described with conventional terminology. To create
the conditions necessary to achieving company and personal goals at the
same time will require a re-orientation of our attitudes, habits, and analytical
methods to structure a framework which will contain all the necessary influences.

In the chapters that follow we shall explore some of the basic concepts of
management planning and control systems and individual performance
planning and review systems and show how goal-setting systems enable
them to support one another. With this base of conceptual understanding we
can then look in detail at some applications of goal setting.

We shall attempt, in short, to answer the question: Exactly what can management do to bring the needs and goals of the company into harmony with
the needs and goals of the individual employee?

The Goal-Interaction Concept

We have seen that company needs give rise to motivation opportunities for
individuals. The trouble is that these opportunities may not be realized by
the very people who should be taking advantage of them because there is no
way to relate company needs and motivation opportunities to individual
needs. Certain motivation media can be provided, and some of these have
already been described. However, we need to develop and keep in mind a
concept of how company and individual goals interact when brought face to
face so that the probability of achieving both is significantly increased.

There are three essential elements in goal interaction: the work itself, the work environment, and the time phasing of individual and organizational goals (Exhibit 8). Basic, of course, is the situation in which the goals of the individual and the goals of the organization are achievable through job content, in which we can provide work that is sufficiently challenging and meaningful; it satisfies individual motivation needs at the same time and by the very same processes that the needs of the company are met.

For example, suppose a manufacturer of the transparent films used in packaging has as a customer one of the biggest commercial bakers in its locality. It establishes an organizational goal which calls for satisfying 50 percent of this particular customer's need for films. Suppose now that it has on its staff a salesman with a strong need for growth, recognition, and achievement. If he has prior knowledge of the company's goal so far as this baker is concerned, then he should be able to establish for himself the personal goal of capturing that part of the market. If he is able to sell the baker an amount of material equal to or greater than the target set by management, he will in turn better himself financially and improve his standing with his superiors.

As another example, take the research scientist in electronics who, like most, enjoys publishing the results of independently performed work. If there is a company need that requires such research within his capabilities, and if company practice will allow publication of the findings in technical journals, our scientist can achieve a personal goal at the same time he

EXHIBIT 8

BASES FOR GOAL INTERACTION

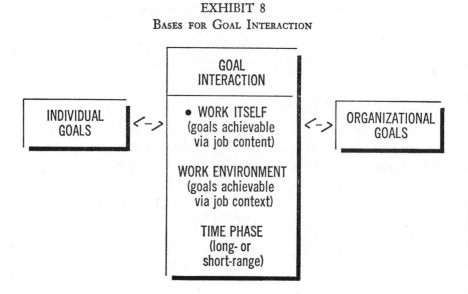

achieves an organizational goal. However, he could also establish a personal goal and work toward it in such a way as to support no company objective. In this second case, individual and organizational goals would fail to interact through the work itself.

In many industrial laboratories, employees in fact pursue research which meets company needs only by accident. For personal goals to support those of the company, and vice versa, instead requires prior knowledge on the part of the individual of the long- and short-range objectives of the organization. However, this knowledge alone does not necessarily mean that the individual can find a company objective that fits his personal goal system. He may know a great deal about future technologies whereas other people in the company have the information on future markets which is needed to set realistic goals. In other words, for effective interaction all the organization's many contributors (considered both as individuals with personal goals and as corporate goal setters) must know each other's tentative aims and seek to relate these through their work.

Some goals, true, are not achievable directly through job content but, rather, must be considered in the context of work environment. In contrast to the work itself with its potential for motivation, the work environment holds more potential for satisfying maintenance needs. Many personal satisfactions can come from membership in the business organization that have nothing intrinsically to do with the job—for example, stimulating social relations. It must also be noted that while not all personal goals can be met through working in an organization, all the goals of the organization must be met through the work of its individual members. Too often management seeks to satisfy organizational goals by turning its employees' attention to the work environment—never realizing that this is a source of great potential dissatisfaction but not a source of motivation.

Then there is the question of time phasing—in other words, long- versus short-range goals. We too often see examples of seriously inadequate time phasing, particularly in cases where people who may be in a job for two years try to work with a one-year budget to achieve a ten-year organizational goal or, alternatively, where individuals are asked to submit plans for the next year's operations before they know what it is the company hopes to achieve.

Education and training can be badly out of phase with personal and company objectives where high-level programs designed to prevent technological obsolescence always seem to be reaching for goals that are years ahead even though immediate company objectives require that a man spend full time on the day-to-day job, thereby blocking his chances for the future. Company planning itself may be so time-consuming that people actually work a ten-month instead of a twelve-month year and spend the other two months planning for the next year's activities and reviewing the year that is not yet finished. This pressure of the short range which interferes with the long range has been referred to as "being so busy cutting grass that we can't stop to sharpen the lawn mower." The proper relationship, in time, between individual and organizational goals can be characterized by an interaction principle which says: "Before I know what *I* am going to do, and before you can know what *you* are going to do, we must first know what *we* are going to do."

In summary, the goal-interaction concept is based upon the idea that the whole is more than the sum of the parts. That is, the sum total of individual goals does not equal the goals of the organization. Conversely, the goals of the organization cannot simply be subdivided and handed to individuals. The nature of the interaction is the source of the increased total which is more than that arrived at merely by adding one part to another. If individual and organizational goals interact effectively, then we have a condition in which both sets become more achievable than they would be separately or out of phase.

The Systems Concept Applied to Goal Setting

A complex entity like the modern corporation cannot spontaneously create an organized system of corporate and personal goals that will interact in the desired manner. This can be achieved only through an understanding of the systems-like nature of human interaction.

A system is the way in which we organize activities in order to achieve a goal. An organizational system is therefore the way in which people are arranged in relationship to each other in order to achieve company objectives. The systems approach to viewing individual and organizational behavior requires managers to re-orient their thinking and perception of the organization in accordance with the systems fundamentals inherent in all behavior, particularly that of people interacting in complex ways to perform complex tasks and achieve complex goals.

The organizational system bears little relationship in fact to the conventional organization chart, which may not represent realistically the way to the achievement of company goals. This is because organizational units are interactive; that is, people in them interact with each other in ways that are not defined and described by formal "boxes" and lines of authority. Research shows that far more time is spent in lateral than in vertical relationships. In other words, we get our work done not so much through the management principles of authority, responsibility, and accountability as through negotiation with people in our same level.

The systems-like nature of the organization arises from the fact that one person cannot get everything done by himself. A management system is therefore the way in which a manager, particularly the president, organizes his work in order to achieve his goals. Everyone cannot report to the chief executive; it is impossible in today's corporation for him to direct everyone's activities. Regardless of the formal organizational chart, the actual work is organized around the objectives, and the achievement of these objectives involves many people in many parts of the company. The organization chart of the future will not describe lines of authority and responsibility in the classical manner, but instead will resemble a systems flow chart which shows the relationship of people and activities to certain defined and specified goals.

Here are some further ideas that will be useful to our understanding of goal-setting systems.

Systems are hierarchical or pyramidal. That is, they are made up of small systems or subsystems that are related by a process or pattern of interaction. The nature of the relationship is determined by the goals sought. Systems assume a hierarchical configuration because this is the efficient manner of organizing; it requires less communication of intelligence among the various parts than any other method of arrangement. This is another way of saying that organizations have information channels with successive levels at which information is consolidated, as a natural way of economizing on time. Unfortunately, the existence of the hierarchy also has the side-effect of minimizing personal interaction.

All systems are a continuum and are not discrete. Each can be viewed as having many subsystems and sub-subsystems and, in turn, as being part of a supersystem. For example, if we consider the corporation to be a system, it has many subsystems: R&D, manufacturing, marketing, finance, personnel, and the like. The corporation also is part of a system made up of other corporations, just as the overall business community is a part of the larger society.

Systems are dynamic, not static. They are constantly changing through the interaction of goals and processes, through the integration of subsystems into larger systems, and through the evolution of these systems into expanded subsystems. The average business firm is constantly re-organizing, and the need for and nature of the re-organization are determined by the success—or lack of it—with which objectives are being achieved. Re-organization is not a "necessary evil" but, in fact, a "necessary good," for unless a system can adapt to changing goals and environment it will become ineffective and useless.

The higher levels of the system control the behavior of the lower levels or subsystems. Objectives are more likely to be determined near the focal point of information and intelligence; that is, at the higher levels of the organizational system rather than the lower levels. This is part of the rationale behind the greater effectiveness of top-down corporate planning. However, we are dealing with a human system, so that control cannot simply take the form of one-way communication of objectives.

With personal goals related only in part to those of the company, the challenge is to develop organizational systems which can accommodate both. In contrast to the "organization man" who has given up all his other relationships, there are numerous examples of human resistance to one-way unilateral control by the management hierarchy. These are easily found in both union and nonunion organizations and in both group and individual reactions, although there is, of course, no such thing as total independence of control. Moreover, it would be mistaken to assume, as management textbooks would have us do, that there is such a thing as unity of command. Owing to the nature of lateral relationships within the business organization, a person in reality has many bosses and is a boss to many people.

The systems concept of organization makes this more understandable as well as more acceptable. Leadership is a function of the people at the focal points of the system, and these focal points are determined by the objectives sought. Behavioral concepts clearly require that the organization be a function of human as well as corporate goals. This is why clarity of purpose is so critical to effective organization and utilization of human resources. The more our goals and the tasks required to achieve them increase in complexity, the more our system will assume a hierarchical character. It is this increase in complexity of goals and activities that has produced the need for decentralization. In a decentralized organization we can have increased participation by individuals in setting and achieving company objectives and still maintain centralized leadership.

There are two basic systems within an organization: planning and control. Planning involves the lateral relationships of the various subunits or subsystems, whereas control involves their vertical relationships. Planning is open-ended; controls are the way in which we "close the loop," obtain feed-back, and measure the extent to which we have achieved our plans. In other words, control follows planning and, while a necessary management system, is not sufficient in itself. Unless plans and goals are effectively determined, controls will be meaningless.

Too many companies establish the control system before the planning and goal-setting system. Also, they neglect to determine whether controls are relevant, valid, and reliable (just the fact that something is easy to measure does not mean it bears any relationship to actual objectives). Then, too, there is the common tendency to forget that control systems signal deviation from plan but do not necessarily correct the indicated problem. The truth of the matter is that management must define the problem further, develop and evaluate alternatives, and select a new goal or plan in order to return the organization to its proper course.

All systems are closed-loop or will become closed-loop over the long range, although management may not determine how or when the loop is closed or even be aware that this has been done. Unless proper feedback loops are pro-vided, people will seek them, whether their own or the organization's per-formance is in question, and the information thus acquired may or may not be relevant.

There are mainstream systems, support systems, and performance-enhanc-ing systems. A mainstream system is one designed to achieve presently known objectives; it is not the one that establishes the goals. In most com-panies the mainstream system has three subsystems corresponding to the cre-ate, make, and market functions. Supporting this are systems which are designed to provide the manpower, money, materials, facilities, and other resources necessary to carry out existing plans. Performance-enhancing sys-tems provide the ways in which the company and its individual members set further goals. Superimposed over mainstream and support systems, they de-termine new and more demanding objectives, strategies for their achieve-ment, and the tactical actions which will make the plans a reality. Per-formance-enhancing systems both precede and follow mainstream activities; in this group we find accounting, quality assurance, industrial engineering, and personnel systems. All, as a matter of fact, can be viewed both as support systems and as performance-enhancing systems. They are support systems when they are supporting present goals, and they are performance-enhancing systems when they bridge the gap between management planning and con-trol and feedback.

The Personnel Management Subsystem

Consider the personnel management subsystem. It is a mechanism for sensing opportunities as well as problems. It collects data from the on-going activities of the enterprise, selects from these data relevant and valid information, and—if the system is properly designed and implemented—converts this information into intelligence useful in problem solving and in capitalizing upon opportunities. It has several subsets of systems: goal setting, work management, communication, compensation, personnel development. It is possible to look at all of these from the standpoint of "Do they provide opportunities for motivation—or for dissatisfaction?" In this way management can identify those which are highly motivational as well as those which hold more potential for dissatisfaction.

The *goal-setting system* can be viewed from the two angles of corporate planning and individual planning. The corporate planning system by which the organization determines its objectives can be an extremely potent motivation opportunity; through individual involvement in it, people's needs for growth, achievement, responsibility, and recognition can be satisfied to a large degree, as can, also, the maintenance needs of orientation and status. Individual performance planning may have many different names in different corporations: performance review, employee appraisal, goal setting, work planning. In any case, individual goal setting will reflect the company's management style. Goal-setting systems are the prime concern of this book and will be dealt with in more detail presently. For the moment let us simply say that they have a strong potential for interaction and that the effectiveness with which they are implemented has a significant influence upon employee motivation.

Work management systems which are self-initiated rather than supervisor-initiated also hold potential for motivation. For example, there is work simplification. Where it is built upon the principle of improvement, by the individual, of the way the job is performed, it satisfies the needs for growth, achievement, responsibility, and recognition significantly—in contrast to work management systems in which standards and methods are conventionally imposed by the supervisor. Without individual interaction in the organization of the work, the opportunity for individual goal setting and achievement is missed.

Then there is the attitude survey, often thought of as simply a way of identifying a problem and invoking management control. When properly designed and administered, this personnel system can have important motivating effects. In many companies the attitude survey is just a way to collect information and opinions which are used by top management as a "club to beat lower management over the head." This raises middle management's anxiety level and increases its psychological pain, which in turn exerts pressure upon first-line supervision to correct the problem that is thought to be present—a short-sighted application indeed of the attitude survey's tremendous potential for motivation. If, however, employees at even the lowest organizational levels know that their views will be listened to and their recommendations acted upon, then they are helping to solve their own as well as the company's problems. Not only does this encourage them to believe that management has their personal needs and goals in mind, but it actually allows those needs and goals to influence those of the company.

In simple terms, the attitude survey should do more than just sample opinion; it is or should be a way of improving work management and promoting a motivating climate. Whether or not it will be effective depends strongly upon the attitudes that management holds about people (Theory X or Theory Y?). If they have the necessary tools and techniques and if the supervisor is competent in interpersonal relations, employees can set their own performance targets and rates of output individually and as a group. This has been demonstrated. Admittedly it is difficult, at least for most supervisors in most companies, but the potential nevertheless still exists.

Communication or orientation systems include all the ways in which information about the company in general, its goals and objectives, its values and purposes, is transmitted to all employees, supervisory and nonsupervisory, at all levels. They can be motivating if they do not sound like Big Brother spreading management propaganda. Communications that have a paternalistic flavor will invariably be rejected by employees; however, those that are sincere, factual, and realistic can be very useful in helping the individual to understand how his role in the company relates to the overall goals. And, remember, communications about specific achievements can be quite as motivating to others as to the individual employee being recognized.

By *compensation systems* we reward people financially for their contribution to company goals. Merit pay, bonuses, profit sharing—these can be either dissatisfying or motivating; their effect depends upon the design and administration of the system. Take, for instance, the description which basically determines the pay for a job. If it is prepared by the supervisor or by a member of the personnel department without any involvement on the part of the individual who is expected to do the job, the effect will be dissatisfaction and demotivation. And a job description which is obsolete is worse than useless; it is, in fact, decidedly detrimental to motivation. In brief, compensation systems which relate individual contribution to company objectives to individual achievement hold tremendous potential for motivation, whereas those which do not discriminate among levels of achievement and contribution can only be sources of disillusionment.

Personnel development systems include training and education of all types, on or off company time and on or off the company premises. They are unique, for they appear to hold only potential for motivation and very little potential for dissatisfaction, provided the employee understands how the training will assist him in achieving his work objectives. Much to management's chagrin, employees sometimes resist development. When this happens, it will usually be found upon analysis that the training does not appear to help the individual in his work at all, or that it relates only loosely to long-term personal goals. On-the-job coaching by the supervisor generally avoids this danger, and so is particularly useful from the standpoint of motivation.

Criteria for Goal-Setting Systems

A degree of freedom is essential to individual goal setting, and company systems and subsystems of the sort described here should provide that freedom. But, if all the members of the organization are to enjoy this freedom, and if their individual goals are to support each other and the goals of the organization as well, these subsystems and sub-subsystems must interact positively with the total system which represents the enterprise as a whole. For this to be possible, the goals of the organization (which are an expression of top management's and especially the chief executive's intentions) must precede individual goals (those of lower-level employees) in time. This is a basic systems concept.

We have noted that systems (that is, organizations) tend to assume a hierarchical or pyramidal arrangement for greatest efficiency. We have also seen that the central or higher-level positions in the hierarchy have the advantage from the standpoint of control. The occupants of these positions must therefore take the initiative in goal setting. They are the leaders; goal setting starts at the control points and moves outward and downward through the organization.

Thus leadership is a requirement of the planning and goal-setting system rather than an executive prerogative. The authority of top management derives, not from inherent power, but from the nature of the systems and subsystems involved. The development of these systems demands, moreover, that the framework of the hierarchy be established before they can be planned efficiently or implemented effectively. To sum up: Management must—

1. Specify company purposes.
2. Break down objectives into subgoals and sub-subgoals until they are stated in terms meaningful to lower-level personnel.
3. Communicate these goals to the subsystems and sub-subsystems of employees (divisions, departments, work units, and so on).
4. Help individual employees to set personal goals through supervisors.
5. Allow for some modification of tentative company goals.
6. Iterate goals and plans for achieving them throughout the hierarchy, recombining and redefining company and personal goals until we reach a balance.

The systems approach makes the goal choices of individuals conditional upon the goals of the corporation. It may or may not be a tough-minded approach. It is authoritarian (Theory X) if we require that individual goals be modified to conform exactly with those of the company. Absolute conformity, obviously, is not the idea at all, nor is it proposed that we do the opposite—that is, subordinate the goals of the company to the goals of the employees (unless we are attempting to run a country club). This is neither intended nor implied by Theory Y.

What *is* implied by a philosophy of management which respects people as individuals and respects their individual needs and goals? It requires, first, that people be willing to adapt to the organization—provided it too will show a degree of adaptiveness. This in turn makes short-range goal choices dependent upon the long range, and it also makes personal goal decisions dependent upon the extent to which the individual moves the person and the company toward organization goals. It calls for adequate feedback from person and company about the probable long-term effects of a particular goal, comprehension of the nature and interdependency of individual and organizational goals, and appropriate feedback about goal achievement which will allow necessary changes to be incorporated in the next planning cycle.

This approach is not really so difficult as it is time-consuming. Yet if, in the long run, people have no chance of achieving personal goals in the company context, the resulting ineffectiveness and conflict will consume much more time. Tedious or not, we must somehow provide management systems which will define goals clearly and assign priorities to them, develop and establish systems for goal interaction, and insure an adequate degree of interpersonal competence on the part of managers, supervisors, and employees alike.

If this sounds difficult, it is necessarily so. However, it is also necessary that management recognize the complexity of today's organization for what it is and deal with it accordingly. Herein we appear to have both an answer and a challenge.

Chapter 11

A General Model
For Goal-Setting Systems

G OAL-SETTING SYSTEMS HAVE A NUMBER OF CHARACTERISTICS IN COMMON. THEY must include, first of all, techniques for planning and, second, techniques for control. That is, an effective goal-setting system must set goals in a hierarchical fashion consistent with systems concepts and also provide techniques for measuring and evaluating the degree of achievement. Once we have determined our general model, we can proceed to examine applications of its concepts to organizational and to individual goal-setting systems and then consider the manner in which these systems interact.

Central Role of Company Purpose

There are several steps in designing a model for goal-setting systems, and they all depend upon the definition of company purpose. This statement must be clearly phrased before goal setting can proceed.

It is not sufficient for the organization or any individual member of it merely to rely upon the fundamental idea of becoming, important though it is. While this is an essential philosophical basis for all the activities, both corporate and individual, that take place within the organization, it is necessary for both individual and company to add a much richer meaning to it. A statement of purpose rightly includes the idea of developing *to the fullest extent possible;* in other words, attempting to become all one has the ability to become.

For an organization the statement of purpose adds appropriate detail to its resolution to "serve the needs of society, customers, and employees through creating, making, and marketing products or services to meet customer needs." Its scope will be as broad or as restricted as the business in which the company wishes to compete within the free enterprise system. It need not be a singular statement but may include several extrapolations and extensions of a central theme.

For the individual, purpose might be defined in terms of his relationship to his family, to society, and to other major influences in his life and—most important—the relationship of his purpose to his concept of himself. Just as we see the company attempting to define what it is by the nature of the business environment, the individual also searches for a definition of who he is.

Individual purpose and company purpose therefore are analogous. The company is made up of individuals and is essentially the expression of individual purposes which find realization through it. Both individual and company must answer in some detail the question of what the ultimate aim or end of all their activities may be—why, in short, certain goals are sought.

The Same Steps and Patterns

Goal setting for the individual and goal setting for the organization follow similar steps and patterns. (See Exhibit 9.) With our purpose clearly defined, we can proceed as follows.

1. *Specific goals to support the stated purpose* must be described in terms of the long and the short range. There must be sufficient detail that they can be communicated meaningfully. This is true whether a department head, for example, is communicating overall company goals to the members of his organization or whether he is communicating his personal goals to other people within the company.

To declare that the first step in goal setting is setting goals is not as circular a statement as might appear at first glance. We find many company managers determining what they are going to do before they have determined what their end purpose is. We also find many managers concerning themselves with problems that they think may arise in the future before they have thought through the relationship of these problems to ultimate objectives. And we find many companies worrying over capital equipment re- placement, electronic data processing, manpower development, and the like before they know what these activities are intended to support.

2. *The importance of these goals* must be spelled out, and *strategy* mapped, as the second step in goal setting. For the individual, goal importance will be expressed in terms of personal motivation; for the company, in terms of motivation of key officers and managers. But for the organization itself it

EXHIBIT 9
THE GOAL-SETTING PROCESS

1. Establishing specific goals to support stated purpose

2. Determining the importance of these goals

3. Making plans for action

4. Arriving at performance standards and measurement criteria

5. Stating anticipated problems

6. Weighing the resources required to carry out the planned action

7. Providing for the interaction of organizational and individual goals

8. Following up with actual performance measurement and evaluation

will be expressed as the relationship between short- and long-range goals and the basic concepts and objectives of the enterprise. What this amounts to is that goals must be analyzed and defined from the standpoint of their contribution to *purpose,* whether individual or organizational.

3. *Plans for action* describe the specific things that will be done in order to achieve the goals. For the company, this step defines the planned program; for the individual, specific responsibilities and the duties entailed. The planned action may involve several hierarchical layers; the range is from broad, generally conceived programs to sharply targeted strategies, and finally to specific descriptions of both corporate (divisional, departmental) activities and job procedures for an employee. These must follow a top-to-bottom sequence because, clearly, the company cannot determine what it will do at the lowest level in the organization until it knows what it is going to do—and why—at the higher levels. In other words, everyone—no matter what his organizational level—must comprehend the plans made at each level above him before he can make his own.

As we move from the broad, generalized plans to the more specific activities, the language used by way of definition may change. It tends to be enriched by the addition of the technologies, specialties, and unique skills of the various groups and their members and by the varied requirements of both. Thus, starting from a general description of the product or service, successive planners describe in greater detail its characteristics, the necessary development work, the market, and a whole series of essential activities.

4. *Performance standards and measurement criteria* follow goals and planned activities. These require the identification of key areas in which results can be measured and definitions of goal achievement. Performance standards for the company may be stated in terms of profit, share of market, capture of certain customers, technological breakthroughs, product cost factors, return on investment, sales and billings, and other such measures of management control. For individual performance, they must indicate the extent to which the person is successful in achieving the stated company objectives. In both cases, however, measurement criteria are derived from goals and must be valid in relationship to them. And, for reliability, an adequate sample of the organization's or the person's performance must be measured to prevent bias.

5. *Anticipated problems* must be stated in recognition of the fact that plans may meet with difficulty, either because of inadequate planning or resources or because conditions change (or a combination of these elements). The problems may be controllable or uncontrollable and will be based upon certain planning assumptions which may remain stable or may change without notice. Alternative approaches to goals should be defined in case the chosen path proves ineffective, inefficient, or impossible; however, such contingency planning must not overshadow mainstream activities to such an extent that there is more concern for remote than for likely possibilities. To anticipate obstacles is to recognize that we live in a probabilistic world and to plan accordingly.

6. *The resources required to carry out the planned action* must be specified. They should not be stated in general terms but must be tied directly to specific goals and subgoals and allocated within the proper time period. For the company, these may include financial support, manpower, equipment and facilities, assistance from other units in the organization, and outside assistance. For the individual, they may take the form of equipment and facilities, training, supervisory guidance, and other assistance needed to achieve goals. At this stage, therefore, budget requirements must be determined, both capital and expense.

7. *Interaction of organizational and individual goals* will be necessary if the target of personal goal achievement through organizational goal achievement is to be met. Beyond involvement and participation this requires care-

ful organization of both company and individual effort. The preceding steps must be performed effectively as they relate to the company before individuals can begin to set their goals and plan their activities.

8. *Actual performance measurement and evaluation* provide the control function. Whether we are judging organizational or individual performance, evaluation must be understood in terms of the results achieved. During this phase the supervisor will have the important task of mediating between individual and organization to help each person understand just how performance has been successful or unsuccessful in relation to objectives.

This general model, then, can be applied to both corporate and personal needs. Its eight steps are obviously relevant to goal setting and planning for the total organization, and they can readily be adapted to provide a system for individual use. Definitely, the two applications have a potential relationship to each other.

Chapter 12

Organizational Goal-Setting Systems

O RGANIZATIONAL GOAL SETTING HAS THE ESSENTIAL INGREDIENTS ALREADY DE-scribed: a clear statement of basic company purpose followed by precisely determined goals to accomplish this purpose, a statement of their importance, plans for action that will identify paths to the goals, performance standards and measurement criteria, consideration of anticipated problems and required resources, interaction of organizational and individual goals, and actual performance measurement and evaluation. In other words, all the conditions which could conceivably affect the achievability of the established goals must be taken into account.

Too many companies think and plan in terms of present conditions. They assume, consciously or unconsciously, that they will continue to operate in the traditional way. Yet an adequate job of goal setting must include a recognition of the need for not only continuity but growth. It must allow for probable changes in environment and in the requirements of shareholders, managers, employees, customers, local and national communities—even, in the case of overseas operations, the international community.

Defining a company's ultimate aim—that is, its purpose—is difficult, particularly since too narrow a definition circumscribes goals and limits opportunities for innovation in the functions of creating, making, and marketing. This is a task which demands of the chief executive and his supporting team of managers all the judgmental ability and creative imagination they can summon up. It requires a weighing of philosophical as well as economic factors. It requires that conflicting interests be reconciled. And it must precede the steps in the goal-setting system which we have outlined in Chapter 11.

1. *Specific objectives.* Whether the company's purpose is expressed in terms of research, manufacturing, marketing, or social responsibility, it must be supported by a statement of the major goals of the enterprise. This at-

tempts to answer the question, "Where are we going and why?" In other words, it represents the long-range ambitions of the company as a whole, over the planned time period, and states the overall objectives from which appropriate subgoals will be measured. It defines the ways in which the firm relates to its environment, uses the available resources, and organizes the work in order to achieve the corporate purpose. In short, it is the initial step in top-down planning. Two stages of subgoal development follow: those concerned with business objectives and business strategies.

Business *objectives* add more meaning to the question, "Where are we going and why?" and are vital to long-range planning and corporate development. They are broad enough to include all the create, make, and market aspects of products and services which have similar markets, technologies, or basic applications of corporate resources. There is a definite time by which they are to be met, and there is an indication of the way they relate to the corporate purpose. They set the parameters for the more detailed subgoals and suggest the direction which planning must take in order to achieve the long-range objectives. And they relate different parts of the corporation through lateral, intercompany planning.

Business *strategies* are the goals of subunits of the organization which move the company toward the business objectives. They might also be called "missions." They define strategic areas, targets, key plans, and long-range checkpoints. Within the limits defined by the specific business objectives, strategies are major sequential courses of action which are broad in concept and scope but are calculated to make a specific contribution to the achievement of the overall goals.

For each specific objective there exist one or more strategies. It is usually necessary for a company to develop several, each discrete in itself, each making a specific contribution toward its own definite objective.

2. *Importance of goals.* It is necessary for managers, during planning, to determine why the established goals are important and answer the question, "How will these strategies lead to the achievement of our long-range objectives?" The possible impact of this step upon the results of the goal-setting effort cannot be overemphasized. Management must be left in no doubt as to how the goals set for this year relate to the company's hopes for the future. Too frequently, various activities go on that do not lead to any predetermined end.

3. *Plans for action.* There must also be tactics and projects, or "sorties," that spell out the detailed tasks of short-range activities. These are the means

to the end. They may be grouped together to support a specific strategy and, even though they are discrete actions, can be summarized into a unified tactical action program.

Tactics and projects show the individual manager how his current activities fit in with overall strategy and indicate the steps by which he must map a path to the goal in question. Here again, it cannot be emphasized too strongly how important it is that the day-to-day, week-to-week, and even year-to-year actions of managers, supervisors, and individual employees tie in absolutely with the firm's long-range strategies and business objectives. This is why planning must be done from the top down—otherwise it will be impossible for management and nonmanagement people alike to know what they should be doing.

Within this framework, defining one's personal work goals (and private goals) creates a significant opportunity for motivation. For, at this level, the majority of the employees can become involved in the corporate planning system. There is usually no problem with higher-level people because they necessarily are involved more intimately in the corporate planning procedure. The challenge to management is to devise systems for extending this opportunity down through the organization—a task which can possibly be accomplished by translating objectives into more meaningful terms through tactics.

There is one exception to the requirement that tactics and projects in all company areas must support company goals: Research and development may of course back up a goal or be purely exploratory (just as it may be both mainstream and staff support). It does not follow that long-range exploratory research operates on an unauthorized, uncontrolled basis—ultimately it must in some way, if successful, contribute to business objectives. However, it will not be the research itself that makes the contribution so much as the programs for action that are set up after the research base is established; rather, research increases the fund of company knowledge, introduces new organizational capabilities, and suggests new opportunities for creating, making, and marketing products or services.

4. *Performance standards and measurement criteria.* Management must next determine how it will know what is being accomplished. Performance standards and measurement criteria answer the question, "How are we going to know when we have reached a goal?" Checkpoints indicate the key result areas and the sequence to be used by managers and other employees in keeping score on their progress. Profit or some derivative thereof will most

likely be the measure of success as reflected in sales volume, cost figures, share of the available market, and so on. Most performance criteria will involve time and dollars.

5. *Anticipated problems.* Any problems anticipated in reaching a goal can be stated as critical comments or as planning assumptions and forecasts. These indicate the activities and areas that must be kept under surveillance and which, if they change, will call for adjustment of goals (strategies) or actions (tactics). Just the fact that a company anticipates problems does not mean literally that it really expects to meet those problems; management is simply determining in advance what maneuvers will be necessary should conditions change or assumptions prove wrong. It is a matter of providing for contingencies, as far as possible, so that goal achievement will not be blocked.

Critical comments may require the development of alternative strategies and, in addition, the naming of a recommended strategy among the alternatives. In some cases there will be parallel strategies which serve the purpose of back-up in the event the recommended strategy turns out, when the need for it arises, to have little probability of success.

6. *Required resources.* The assistance required to carry out planned action includes both money and manpower. Therefore, in estimating costs, management must take into account salaries, materials, equipment, and overhead related directly or indirectly to the plan. It must also identify whatever capital must be committed. And since, in the large corporation, many activities are decentralized, it is necessary to have a clear understanding of the assistance required from other parts of the organization. In summary, this step gives us a detailed indication of what we have to have to get where we want to go.

7. *Interaction of organizational and individual goals.* Employees at all levels must be thoroughly familiar with the corporate planning system if they are to be successful in achieving their personal goals through the achievement of company goals. Simple participation, as we have seen, is not the answer; rather, it is meaningful involvement in the organizational goal-setting system itself that creates the motivation to achieve. In a subsequent chapter we shall explore this organizational and individual goal interface in some detail. From the standpoint of organizational goal setting, let us simply say that all planning activity must be confirmed and charters established for responsible individuals and groups to proceed toward objectives.

In some corporations this is done in long-range planning and annual planning conferences in which key people who are responsible for strategies have their goals and plans reviewed by top management. However, this sort of review cannot in fact be left to a big conference of top-level managers; instead, meetings must be held regularly to involve smaller groups of individuals in the whole process of developing strategies at all levels. In the final stage the iteration of organizational goals serves to promote the best possible balance of strategies and tactics as the validity and reliability of plans are measured against the judgment of management. After the necessary adjustments have been made, each part of the organization communicates its intentions to the others so that everyone can have the overall picture.

8. *Actual performance measurement and evaluation.* This is the point at which the yardsticks developed in Step 4 are applied to determine the degree to which goals have been met. Obviously management cannot wait until time has run out before checking on the progress made. Review may be scheduled on a calendar basis (monthly, quarterly, or annually) or according to the timetable established for a particular objective or strategy. The validity of measures depends on management's perception, direct evidence (control and accounting), staff audits, management systems, and plain honesty.

To the extent that individual goals are correlated and phased with those of the organization, the measurement of individual performance can be achieved at the same time and by the same process. Here the results-oriented philosophy of management by objectives achieves its fullest fruition and here, also, the benefits of organizational goal setting are realized most concretely. Here both organization and individual look back upon their accomplishments (or the lack of them), measure the extent of their success, and consider the activities that contributed to or detracted from that success. Such an analysis, not only of the results achieved but of the means employed in achieving them, can then be put to good use in the next goal-setting cycle.

Chapter 13

Individual Goal-Setting Systems

LET US NOW CONSIDER THE APPLICATION OF THE GENERAL GOAL-SETTING MODEL TO the individual. Like organizational goal setting, individual goal setting parallels the model closely through the eight steps. It starts with a statement of purpose—in this case, the human purpose of becoming. Every individual needs to grow psychologically, and he expresses this purpose in his efforts to expand and enrich his concept of himself, to discover who he is as a person. In other words, his purpose has origins similar to that of the organization. After all, organizational purpose is simply an extension of the thinking of those key individuals who have most influence on the direction corporate development will take.

1. *Specific objectives.* The achievement-oriented person who constantly seeks goals must define his career objectives as well as his immediate, shorter-range tasks and work objectives. This may be done at the time of a periodic performance review, generally on an annual or semiannual basis and possibly as part of a personnel management system of performance planning.

It is the thesis of this book, once more, that to establish personal goals it is necessary for the individual to have prior knowledge of the organization's goals; otherwise the two will not be harmonious. Neither company nor individual can long tolerate a condition in which personal goals do not relate in some way to those established for the organization. Whatever the individual does at work must fit in; he must be able to perceive himself as a person seeking career objectives, and he must find these objectives within the company, or else he may choose or be forced to leave and seek them in another environment. However, it is not enough for him to establish long-range objectives without considering the intermediate targets that will provide discrete steps to his ultimate end. He should have his private system of goals analogous to the company's objectives, business objectives, and strategies, and they should take the same hierarchical form—or at least they should if he is to get what he wants out of life.

The ambitious man, moreover, will establish these personal goals with the idea of achieving them with a degree of excellence, not just perfunctorily. Like the company, he will address himself seriously to the question, "What do I want to become?" And his more immediate missions will tell him how to get there in the same way that business tactics define means for the organization.

2. *Importance of goals—motivation.* Again, just as the company spells out the reasons why certain goals and subgoals are important and determines how the proposed strategies will support them, in like manner the individual must reaffirm his goals and review his strategies. He must be persuaded that his goals will meet his needs for achievement, growth, recognition, and responsibility. In simple terms, he must *want* to reach them. Therefore, in establishing and documenting his goals and in communicating them to his supervisor, he must consider the *why* of his intentions.

Research on personal goal setting has shown that there is no substitute for a definite statement, either written or spoken, in which the person makes a commitment not only to others who depend upon his actions but to himself. Through this commitment motivation as well as communication is achieved. It is easy to find employees who are highly articulate about why they want to do something, but cannot say precisely what it is they want to do or how it will serve either their own ends or the objectives of the company. Obviously, true commitment requires careful consideration and thought on the part of the individual, but it is well worth the effort in terms of a successful career.

3. *Plans for action.* The action planned by the individual describes in detail the step-by-step process he will use to reach his and the company's goals. This sort of effort is often skimped. All managers are aware that while people may have an objective in mind and appear motivated to achieve it, in many cases they have not considered what may be necessary to move them in that direction.

The goal seeker, it will be remembered, is more likely to be motivated to achievement if he has independent responsibility for determining the precise action he will take. Supervisor- and management-initiated job descriptions therefore do not satisfy him; on the contrary, so far as he is concerned they can only be sources of dissatisfaction.

4. *Performance standards and measurement criteria.* Yardsticks and target dates must be determined before the work has actually been finished; other-

wise it will be impossible for the individual to know when he has done a good job. This is particularly important for the highly motivated goal seeker who, with his strong need for feedback about his progress, always wants to know how "the game will be scored." If we leave the establishment of performance standards until the end of the work period, we deny him one of the significant factors in motivation.

Performance standards may be stated in company or in individual terms; however, the employee must understand them in his own terms and know exactly how he will be measured, else measurement has no point. Standards which are felt to be arbitrary, capricious, or unrelated to goals will be sources of frustration, and measurement may then become something to be avoided. One reason why the task-oriented person shuns evaluation is that he has learned from life to expect that measurement of his performance will be essentially unrelated to the results he achieves.

It should hardly be necessary to repeat that standards must be firmly based upon results and contribution to company objectives, certainly not upon personality characteristics and only secondarily upon the process by which they are achieved. If the way in which a goal is reached becomes important—and, under some conditions, it may—the fact that this is to be used as a criterion must be spelled out.

It is feasible to permit and even encourage the individual to set his own criteria for achievement. A word of caution may be in order, however. Because it is a characteristic of motivated people to set more difficult standards for themselves than would ordinarily be set by their superiors, the supervisor may have to be prepared to coach the person to avoid overcommitment.

5. *Anticipated problems.* The individual must recognize that there will be barriers to achieving his goals. These obstacles in his way may be personal or organizational.

Personal obstacles relate to one's capabilities as an individual; to aptitudes, training, education, on-the-job experience, personality and temperament, and—particularly important—factors and prejudices affecting job placement. Some personal barriers can be removed by additional training, so long as it relates specifically to performance which is necessary to reach goals, and others may be alleviated to a significant degree by a change of job assignment. We must recognize, however, that there are also some personal barriers which, so far as business life is concerned, are not correctable. Seriously inadequate training may be an insurmountable handicap in view of the time and money required to overcome it, and a person will be able to do little, with or without help, to correct inherent deficiencies such as limited intelligence or lack of special aptitudes, although sometimes these barriers can be planned around strategically.

There are also personality factors which may or may not be controllable and changeable by the individual with or without assistance. Most companies are not in the business of psychotherapy, but most managers may at some time be forced to "live" with difficult personality traits in one or more subordinates. This they do by change of assignment, special supervision, or informal counseling.

The No. 1 company barrier for most individuals is lack of opportunity for advancement beyond a certain point. The number of top jobs within a given organization is limited; not every deserving candidate can expect to grow indefinitely in status and responsibility. The situation will be somewhat more fluid in a company that itself is growing and so must constantly be on the look-out for new talent, but there can be no guarantee that a higher position will be waiting for a man when he is ready for it and he may have to consider a change of company to further his career. However, an apparent opportunity barrier is often created by lack of information about the company's plans and objectives, so that personal goal setting is blocked. And still other problems may be caused by supervisors, their superiors, and fellow employees, as well as by inadequate tools, materials, and other resources.

Of course the goal seeker who is alert to obstacles that may stand in his way can often find ways to circumvent them and still reach his objectives. There are "jungle fighters" who can survive in the organizational underworld in spite of all the barricades erected by the company system either consciously or unconsciously. However, these barriers characteristically produce a situation in which the needs for growth, recognition, responsibility, and achievement cannot be satisfied. For this reason it is up to management to be alert to organizational inadequacies on the one hand and its role in providing motivation opportunities and media on the other.

6. *Required assistance.* No one achieves his goals entirely by himself; invariably he has some degree of assistance from others. In addition to his associates, his supervisor, and higher management, this assistance may come from members of other departments or even from outside sources. Much of it will take the form, in other words, of cooperation; that is, it will be interpersonal in nature. (We assume that the necessary equipment, facilities, and financial support will be forthcoming.) Hence the importance of understanding the objectives and goals of others. Some people do not like to ask for help, but the fact that everyone needs and uses it must be recognized.

7. *Organizational and individual goal reaction.* Ideally, the goals of the individual and the goals of the organization should interact so effectively that all become more achievable. In this way we can add one and one and get something more than two. The nature of this interaction will be covered in more detail in the next chapter.

8. *Actual performance measurement and evaluation.* Our cycle of individual goal setting started with goal setting and performance planning—that is, with performance preview. Now it is completed by the application of the established performance standards to measure the degree to which both work and personal goals have been achieved. At this point the next cycle of individual goal setting begins.

In the process of interaction, one hopes, individual goals will be reconfirmed and the employee's charter to proceed will be established. Depending upon his level in the organization, he may participate in annual and long-range corporate planning meetings. Since, however, not everyone can share personally in these sessions, the interaction of his goals with those of the company must be facilitated by some other means. (This problem, too, will be treated in Chapter 14.)

The success of the performance review discussion between employee and supervisor will depend on the interpersonal competence of both, but particularly the supervisor. His role here is essentially that of a mediator between the individual and the organization; that is, he aids in the effective implementation of both the individual and the organizational goal-setting system. There is, moreover, a singularly important concept which he must keep in mind throughout this discussion and, in fact, during the entire evaluation process. It is the way in which he determines the extent to which the employee has become a true goal seeker. *Goal setting has been done when the individual knows what he expects of himself, not just what management expects of him.*

Chapter 14

Individual and Organizational
Goal Interaction

W E HAVE NOW LOOKED AT INDIVIDUAL AND ORGANIZATIONAL GOAL-SETTING
systems in some detail. But do we know exactly how these two mecha-
nisms should and do relate to each other? This is something that is difficult to
communicate and most difficult to implement. There may be some cases in
American industry where the necessary interaction occurs effectively, but apparently these are quite isolated. Yet the coming era of management requires
that we learn how to create the proper conditions for goal setting and
achievement motivation—a tremendous challenge that deserves recognition
and acknowledgment on the part of all who claim managerial authority and
responsibility.

Both Systems and People Failures

Let us begin by looking at some of the reasons why effective interaction
does *not* occur.

First of all, either the individual or the organizational system can fail as a
separate entity. In addition, people can fail to implement a good system satisfactorily. The purist in systems theory may say that there is no such thing as
a "people failure," that there are simply systems failures. This is partly true
since, if a system fails, it is almost certain that the people will fail too.

In this book we have presented the idea of systems interaction in which
the individual and the organizational goal-setting system have a definite relationship provided by the systems themselves. They have a common point
of contact in which management and employee can identify the way in
which each is to interact in the setting of goals. This assumes a perfect or

near-perfect system in both cases. While, however, there are many excellent organizational goal-setting systems, American industry has yet to produce a really effective individual goal-setting system even though the basic concepts are sufficiently well known at this time.

To be "perfect" for our purposes, the two systems should have clear interfaces. But, if we look around us, we will readily see that systems usually do not interface well, that each must be interpreted or translated into the other's terms. The question then becomes: How is this translation (or mediation) accomplished?

There are two ways in which this can be done: one effective, the other ineffective. The ineffective management technique is simply to transmit, not translate. "Transmission" implies a mere restatement of company goals in company terms, whereas "translation" involves relating both goals and strategies to the individual's job situation. In other words, "goal setting has been done when the individual knows what he expects of himself, not just what management expects of him."

This brings the supervisor into the picture. For, as management has recognized for some time, it is the supervisor who gets the company's work done through people—which is another way of saying that the supervisor interprets and translates the company goals for the individual. If he does it unilaterally, we will have demotivating conditions; however, if he does it on a bilateral basis, we may have conditions that are conducive to motivation. As we have said repeatedly, what is needed is more than participation; the company goals must be turned into another language, another set of symbols, that will be meaningful to the individual.

That is why we say that the conditions necessary for effective interaction of individual and organization are *clear meaningful goals, understandable and helpful goal-setting systems, and management interpersonal competence.* The distinction between Theory X and Theory Y becomes critically important, as does management's understanding of achievement motivation and goal seeking. Even with effective systems interaction—that is, clear interpretation and translation—a supervisor who practices Theory X blocks motivation opportunities. The bulk of the employees, particularly those at lower levels, know little if anything about the thinking and working of top management. Even if its members are sincerely concerned for the well-being of their people as individuals, and even if their goals for the enterprise are translated into the appropriate language and handed down in written form, by word of mouth, and by conscious example, there will be little incentive to individual goal setting if participation in work planning is denied and the whole concept of motivation is contradicted by authoritarian behavior on the part of the man at the bottom of the management pyramid.

But now let's look at the opposite extreme. We can have the most effective, Theory Y-oriented supervisor conceivable; however, he may still be ineffective in translating the goals of the organization to the individual worker. Why? Because of the inadequacy of the company planning system or of higher-level management.

In summary, we can have both "systems failures" and "people failures" in goal setting. Or we can have effectiveness in one but not in the other system if the phasing and interrelation of the two do not take proper account of the systems nature of the enterprise. The flow-diagram approach to organization charting should become increasingly important in developing the necessary understanding because it shows this systems nature graphically and indicates the timing of the various aspects of goal setting and operations.

Management, supervisors, employees—every member of the organization should, in fact, understand to some degree the basic nature of human systems and, specifically, the nature of company and individual goal-setting systems as they relate to one another. This signals a change of emphasis in management and supervisory training away from "human relations" and toward the systems approach. It also signals the increasing need for a more open and honest "leveling" with everyone in the organization about purposes, objectives, and goals.

Teams and Team Balance

Managers often think about groups of persons as teams. These may be groups of management, supervisory, or nonsupervisory employees. The problem is not so much in assembling a team as in balancing the abilities of the individual team members in order to best achieve the stated objectives.

A team is not a committee. It is not simply an additional layer of management, and it is not a manager and his staff assistants. In other words, a team is not a simple functional arrangement of activities, nor is it an extension of the team leader himself. More than the sum of the individual members, in a sense it is a smaller model of the entire organization. A team is a group of individuals working together for the same goals—that is, the goals of a part of the overall organization.

The purpose of the team approach is to increase the ability of one focal point of organization planning and control (for instance, a profit center or an entrepreneurial-type subsystem within the company) to achieve specific goals by sharing them among two or more people at the same level who support the same manager or contribute to the same objectives. Team members may or may not be in the same formal organizational unit; the team may, in fact, cross classical departmental lines. That is, it has a systems characteristic, its structure being determined by the goals to be met. Team balance is the key whereby the best mix of abilities, aptitudes, experience, and know-how is structured in the manner that will be most conducive to achieving objectives.

Balancing a team is admittedly difficult, but it is becoming more and more important as companies move closer to the systems approach to management. There are several questions that must be answered: (1) What are the team's goals? (2) What individual competences are needed on the team? (3) How does a manager relate the abilities of individuals to get the optimal balance? and (4) How does a manager do all these things and still satisfy the growth needs of the individuals concerned?

The concept of team balance cannot be imposed on an organization that does not have an adequate planning system for defining company goals and a system for encouraging the setting of individual goals. Team goals are an expression of unity of purpose within an organizational unit. They may be simply extensions of the leader's objectives, but they can be more than that. They do require a good job of organizational goal setting and a good job of personal goal setting on the part of the team leader.

The usual method of organizing a team, particularly a management team, is the writing of man specifications. This is a sterile and inadequate approach because it assumes that an individual adapts to what has been placed on paper and molds himself to a prestructured job. Any management team worthy of the name will reject individuals who are willing to do this, and any manager who deserves a place on a key team is unlikely to accept such an assignment. In other words, the team is not an attempt to subordinate the needs of individual members to the needs of the leader. Skills and experience and motivation come in "whole man" units, and management cannot attempt to select and assemble team members the way one would custom-order and build a machine. The problem is not unlike that of assembling a jigsaw puzzle in which we have a finite number of precut pieces, some of which do not fit together precisely.

Many managers have a tendency to select subordinates in their own image; that is, to staff their team with people who are like themselves. This is neither a healthy nor an effective approach to organizing and balancing a team. It is not healthy because of what it can do to individuals, and it is not effective because we cannot build a goal-achieving organization with identical people. The criteria for a balanced team do not require that each individual member be a miniature team unto himself; the necessary abilities must be present, not within each person, but within the overall group.

For the same reasons that make position specifications sterile, a team is not static but, rather, is dynamic. Every time the organizational goals change or team members are replaced or grow as individuals, rebalancing must occur. In fact, rebalancing is a constant process rather than a one-time proposition, and the leader must be forever sensitive to the need for re-establishing team balance. He can achieve the best balance feasible at a point in time only by establishing the overall team goals first. Then he must search inside and outside the company for individuals who have both the abilities and the personal goals that will fit in.

Balance is not arrived at by adding up individual goals and abilities and somehow establishing goals on this basis. It is not achieved by stating the team's goals and then forcing the individual members into the predetermined structure. It requires careful adjustment of all its elements.

The N-Person Team

A team may have any number of members: two, three, four, or *n*. The simplest case, of course, is the two-person team. The probable balance is clearest in this small group, and the problem of balance can be stated as just this: Can both team members get what they want while performing tasks that are mutually dependent and still achieve organizational objectives? The goal-setting approach points to the necessity of having team (organizational) goals in addition to the individual goals. Otherwise there is no basis for the satisfaction of personal needs, much less the meeting of organizational objectives and needs. If imbalance is indicated, one of four corrective measures will be required: (1) replacing Member A, Member B, or both; (2) causing A or B (or both) to modify their personal goals; (3) modifying team goals; or (4) moving the team to another place in the organization.

With teams of three, four, or *n* people, the problem increases factorially. It is easy to see why this is one of the most difficult and challenging management responsibilities. The only hope for effective performance on the part of the large team is the same as for the total organization—because, in fact, the company *is* a very large team. Unity of purpose and objectives is the key.

The leader may deal with his team according to Theory X or Theory Y. Indeed, these two philosophies will indicate two different approaches to establishing and balancing a team in the first place. If the leader takes the Theory X approach, he will assume that the team members are incapable of self-initiated behavior and that he must control them. In this case we find the manager-leader acting as an intermediary for all his subordinates and the organization, determining all individual objectives and team objectives, exercising close supervision, and requiring only group action. It is this method of management that has, to some extent, been back of the alarm about the "organization man," and certainly it is a serious mistake for a leader to try to manipulate the behavior of the team as a total group rather than as individuals.

Manipulative managers attempt to force their people to fit predetermined man specifications and job descriptions. They put the jigsaw puzzle together by suppressing or cutting off parts of the pieces if they do not "belong." In contrast, the manager who takes the Theory Y approach does not attempt to reshape individual team members to fit his grand plan, but rather accepts or rejects team members who belong or do not belong and so establishes an effective balance. The best team, with the best balance, is the one that gets results and achieves the team's goals; even so, however, the leader may deliberately structure his team with less than optimal immediate balance to help individual members broaden their experience and thereby contribute more effectively to ultimate long-range balance.

In an *n*-person team the leader is dealing with a dynamic situation in which goals change, the members change, and sometimes the leader changes. He cannot expect to assemble a team, balance it, and then step back and watch it function smoothly. He must make up for the gaps in the members' skills and experience—for in any growing organization there will always be some gaps—and for their interpersonal incompetence. In a word, he must use himself to achieve balance. This does not mean settling arguments by the exercise of his authority or by the removal of team members, although either or both may be necessary in some cases. Rather, it implies a more developmental approach to the job of helping individuals work together effectively. Clearly, therefore, the team leader must himself be skilled in interpersonal effectiveness, and he must also have a keen awareness of and sensitivity to individuals and their needs.

All the concepts and principles of individual and organizational goal setting apply very obviously to the problem of establishing team balance (as they do to the overall management job). This will, in fact, be their most frequent application. For the organization is comprised of as many teams as there are systems of goal setting and achievement.

Chapter 15

Abilities and Performance

THE PERSONAL EQUATION MUST BE FACTORED INTO THE PLANS OF BOTH ORGANI-
zation and individual. We have seen that the motivation of an employee
to reach and set work goals is always a key concern of management, as well as
of the individual himself. So too is the ability to perform the necessary
tasks, whose relationship to effective performance on the job is so direct as to
leave no question. While no amount of personal ability can overcome inadequate goal setting, goals in themselves are not sufficient. Know-how and skill
do in the end determine whether a man will achieve lasting success. Thus
motivated work behavior and ability come together to produce effective
performance—provided goals and abilities correlate.

The unique capabilities of the individual employee depend on three factors: (1) aptitudes, (2) experience, and (3) placement. All three contribute to his net effectiveness. (See Exhibit 10.)

Aptitudes

Aptitudes have been conceived by psychologists in many ways. For our
purposes we shall consider a simple model which includes two main compo-
nents: capacity and temperament.

Capacity includes all the mental and physical aptitudes of an individual
that are present at the time he is expected to do his work. Included are intelligence (which comes in many kinds and sizes) and basic drive or energy
level. Capacity, in other words, is a person's inherent aptitude for learning. It
has nothing to do with *what* has been learned, but is an estimate of ability to
acquire skills and know-how.

The other component of aptitude is *temperament,* which includes both
real and apparent factors of personality and behavior patterns. Why should

we consider personality a factor in aptitude? Because managers and supervisors will have little influence over it in the work situation—essentially it develops during childhood and early adulthood and, while not completely unchangeable, is well formed at the time of employment.

The inability of the organization to change those mental qualities which are either inherent or acquired early is generally recognized; however, management often attempts to modify the personalities of employees. We find this occurring during performance appraisals in which supervisors feed back to the individual the "facts" about his behavior and attitudes with the expectation that, with this information about himself, he will "improve." If it

EXHIBIT 10
FACTORS AFFECTING ABILITIES

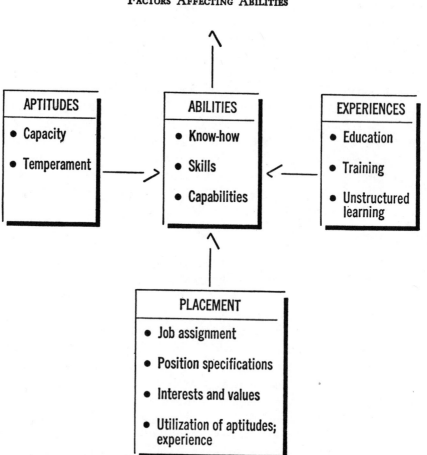

were not that he has spent 20 or 30 years and more learning how to be who and what he is, there might be some hope of effecting changes in a personality pattern detrimental to effective performance. But, as a general rule of thumb, it takes a person as long to unlearn old patterns of behavior and learn new ones as it did for him to acquire the old ones in the first place. Thus the supervisor and the organization (and the employee, for that matter) simply do not have the time—even if they had the capacity—to engage in quasi-psychotherapy. What everyone should be concerned about, on the other hand, is the extent to which we can comprehend people's capacities and temperaments and design jobs and organizations with these in mind so that, whatever the aptitudes of individual employees, goal achievement is possible.

Many companies use tests to evaluate the capacities and even the temperaments of prospective employees with the objective of selecting those people who seem best suited to the work to be done. Much has been written, both pro and con, about so-called psychological testing in particular, and there is no need here to review the literature in this field. We can sum up most of what has been said in the idea that psychological tests, like measurement tools in nonhuman areas, are no better than the people who use them. Much individual judgment is required to interpret the test results; there are several potential sources of error. However, if management will keep in mind the same sort of reservations it has about other measuring instruments, recognizing the limitations of statistical sampling, it will have an adequate understanding of the problems associated with effective personnel testing.

Especially important, as with all testing devices, are the problems of reliability and validity. That is, will we get the same results another time, and do we know what they mean? We must recognize also that tests of aptitude measure essentially *prior* learning and that additional education and training might very well change the test scores. Should, therefore, companies be concerned at all with the aptitudes of employees? Of course they should, since these have such an obvious bearing upon the ability of an individual to do his job. The point—to repeat—is simply that tests supplement, they do not supplant, managerial judgments.

Apart from cultural determinants a person's potential varies as a function of physical drive, intelligence, and personality, all of which affect considerably the kinds of things that he does well. Whether or not they are born in the person or acquired, they are enhanced or depressed by the experiences and opportunities he has had for learning. The more a person learns, in fact, the more he seems able to learn. For instance, individuals who come from deprived environments tend to score lower on tests of aptitude and to show more personality problems, but when they are exposed to an environment richer in opportunities for new learning, their aptitudes often increase and their psychological symptoms lessen.

Employees come to a company after many years of learning, and to a degree their aptitudes are already "set." It is clear, however, that as long as they continue to learn, their aptitudes—or ability to learn—will be maintained. This is why we attach such importance to exposure to new learning at work and placement of the individual within a job where he can apply his learning. What we must ask when considering a prospective employee's ability is this: Given his capacity and temperament, is he likely not only to achieve effective job performance within a reasonable time but to learn and grow as the job grows?

Experience

We have included experience as one factor in teaching a man to be the kind of person he is. This is one type of experience. Now we turn to another variety—that relating to education, training, and something we can call unstructured learning. As with aptitudes, much of all this has been acquired prior to the time the person becomes an employee. Some education and training, however, are transferable, though some we wish were not! That is, what is learned from one set of experiences is applicable in another situation. The degree of transfer will depend upon the degree to which the present job situation is like an earlier one or the degree to which the tasks required of the person relate to his formal education or training.

This, then, is what management must be constantly concerned with in hiring or transfer: How closely does this man's past experience relate to his present (or proposed) job assignment? For an answer to this question, we must look to the goals that have been set for that job, as well as the individual tasks to be performed, and estimate the amount of correlation. Experience is usually additive; that is, once we have learned something, it is not likely that we will forget it, particularly if we have been using what we have learned. Thus, while related experience in a former job may help in the new one, we must also recognize the fact that past experience may very well interfere with performance in the new situation if what the employee learned as "the right way" in the past is now considered to be wrong. In other words, not all training is transferable in a positive sense; some will be a handicap to effective performance even though, on the surface, it appears relevant.

Supervisors sometimes say they would rather have a new, "green" employee than an old, experienced one because they can teach him the right way to do things. While there is some validity to this idea, it is obviously impractical to have to start from the beginning every time we train someone. If, on the other hand, we are hiring a salesman, not just any salesman will do. Marketing in one industry or business is not necessarily the same as in another; in fact, experience in an unrelated sales job may preclude the desired performance in a new position. When it comes to education and training, in short, we must look beneath the surface and behind the label attached, whether it be that of draftsman, machinist, or salesman or a bachelor's degree in electrical engineering.

Let's consider engineering for a moment. Engineering in one company is by no means always engineering in the next. Not only are the objectives and techniques of the work likely to be different, but so are the standards of performance. Management has not defined its goals well enough if it simply seeks graduates in electrical or chemical engineering, for example, without looking at some of the fields in which a student may specialize and the possible variations in the quality and type of the training received. A sizable portion of the education gained in our public high schools and our colleges and universities is simply not applicable to the business organization; and although we are beginning to see some improvement in this respect, it will be another generation before this has a significant effect. Meanwhile, we must look at an individual's background in depth as it relates to company objectives.

All learning should include "learning how to learn." The legendary self-made or self-taught man is in reality not so rare as supervisors sometimes think, because everyone actually is self-made by his individual responses to the opportunities he has had. In other words, experience interacts with aptitudes as two of the key factors contributing to his abilities. And it should be said, too, that with a given set of aptitudes, human beings are capable of gaining considerably more from experience than most of us do.

If we think of education as a structured learning process which has been directed toward general goals, then training can be thought of as a learning process which is more structured and is directed toward very specific goals. Besides these two, there is also unstructured learning, which is more random and gets its structure from the learner's frame of reference. Unstructured learning occurs constantly, on the job as elsewhere, but it can have meaning to the individual only if he has adequate preparation—that is, a frame into which he can fit what he is learning from day to day. Many jobs do not require structured education and training, but on-the-job experience is not invariably adequate training for employees. It can be a good teacher only if the goals of the job are sufficiently understood that it is obvious to the employee how what is going on around him relates to what he himself is doing.

The developing field of programed instruction holds significant clues for on-the-job training. A fundamental concept here is the specification of "terminal behaviors." This is simply a way of saying that before we start teaching a person to do anything we must adequately define what he will be expected to do when the training is finished. Then we proceed to develop a step-by-step system for reaching that objective. This concept clearly has much in common with that of goal setting—as indeed it should, because the two have overlapping objectives.

Placement

Regardless of what aptitudes and experience the employee may have, effective job performance will not result unless he is in a position to apply what he knows. The key factors to be considered under placement are job assignment, the requirements of the job, interests and values, and the degree to which aptitudes and experience can be utilized.

Any job assignment which is to produce the ability to perform a task *must* consider aptitudes and experience. These may be translated into job requirements—with the caution that position specifications are relevant only to a particular job at a particular time and serve only to locate and identify a prospective employee. They cannot indicate to the individual or his supervisor how the job is to be done; they simply state the minimum level of skills and know-how required to perform the necessary tasks and achieve appropriate work goals.

The individual's natural interests and personal value system also are of considerable importance, for unless they are satisfied, motivation cannot persist for long. The question is, however, which comes first: interest in a job or the performance of that job? We often hear the statement that we do well what we like to do, but in actuality this reverses the process. Rather, we become interested in, and include in our value system, those things that we know well. First we learn how to do something or learn about it; then we determine our level of interest. It is impossible for either an employee or his supervisor to judge adequately whether he will be interested in a particular job until both know whether he understands it.

If we will consider what we know about goal seeking, we will remember that we can develop interest in any activity which leads us to the achievement of our personal goals. Many people express disinterest in a certain kind of work—often because they know next to nothing about it but often, too, because they have been unsuccessful in reaching their personal goals through it. Yet an employee's attitude toward a particular type of job can change if he discovers that it will satisfy his motivation needs for achievement, recognition, growth, and responsibility.

Placement, in brief, must consider both aptitudes and experience and strive for the particular combination of these in a job assignment that will utilize them satisfactorily. The three factors, properly balanced, will produce the ability to work effectively, but not even overwhelming ability will produce effective performance without adequate goal setting and motivation.

Chapter 16

A Total System for Motivation

MOTIVATION REQUIRES A COMBINATION OF ALL THE SYSTEMS AND SUBSYSTEMS described thus far. The important concept included in this combination system is the human purpose of becoming and its expression in both individual and company terms, leading to the definition of customer and company needs for products and services as well as individual motivation needs for achievement, growth, recognition, and responsibility. The customer-company needs give rise to motivation opportunities through the attempts of the organization to assure continuity and growth, not only for itself but for all its members. The individual motivation needs can be satisfied by the organizational system through motivation media which include opportunities for personal growth related to organizational growth.

The apparently divergent paths of individuals and organization can be reconciled when we consider the process of goal setting. Goal-setting systems for both relate the needs of the company to the needs of its employees and facilitate positive interaction. Goal setting then becomes a key to individual and organizational effectiveness.

One of the prime requisites of effective individual goal setting is prior knowledge of and involvement in the establishment of organizational objectives and the strategies planned in support of them. This prior knowledge and this involvement enable the employee to tie his own goals in with the organization's. (The systems nature of this interaction is shown in the flow chart reproduced as Exhibit 11.) Result: motivated work behavior.

Next let us review briefly what we have said about individual ability and the factors that contribute to it: aptitudes, experience, and placement. While effective individual and organizational goal setting plays an important part in creating the right conditions for motivation, ability must join with the work itself in order to produce effective performance. And it is effective per-

EXHIBIT 11
Motivation System

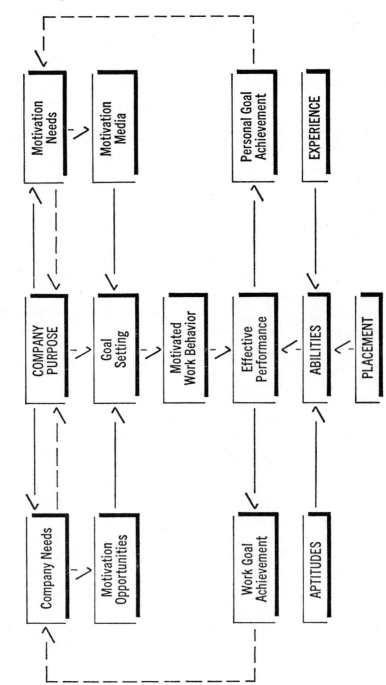

formance that leads to work goal achievement as well as personal goal achievement.

If we were to remove goal setting from the flow chart in Exhibit 11—that is, fail to provide for the interaction of individual and organizational goals —then we could expect conflict between the purposes of the organization and those of its members. The goal-setting systems, however, bring them into alignment.

Thus the systems approach holds significant potential for the company management whose philosophy calls for permitting and—more—encouraging its people to work together to achieve organizational goals in a manner that will also enable them to achieve their private goals. The success with which this concept is implemented will depend, as we have seen, upon the ingenuity of all concerned, not just in restating company goals for employee consumption, but in interpreting and translating them into terms meaningful to the individual at whatever level he may be—and, conversely, translating the personal goals of this individual into work goals that will support the company's aims and objectives.

The role of the supervisor—and indeed of all managers—in this total goal-setting system is self-evident.

PART FOUR

Final Thoughts

Chapter 17

The Role of Maintenance Needs

THE CONCEPT OF MAINTENANCE NEEDS WHICH WE INTRODUCED IN CHAPTER 4 has to do with the individual's concern for his environment. Maintenance needs depend for their fulfillment on the "friendliness" of the environment (or its hostility). For employees, the job context is the environment that "maintains."

Maintenance needs are more physical in nature than motivation needs, which are more psychological. Exhibit 3 of Chapter 4 describes other essential differences between the two as well. Maintenance needs cannot be sources of satisfaction; they can only produce dissatisfaction or, at best, avoid it. In other words, the most that management can hope to achieve through satisfying its employees' maintenance needs is the absence of discontent and unhappiness. Even maximum satisfaction of maintenance needs, up to the full level of the employees' expectations, does not lead to effective performance in the same way that motivation needs affect job performance. But, if maintenance needs are not kept at "par," the dissatisfaction that results may definitely affect performance.

Motivation needs and maintenance needs are partially independent of one another. That is, an employee can be both satisfied with motivation factors in his work and dissatisfied with its maintenance factors at the same time. For example, he can be satisfying his needs for achievement, growth, responsibility, and recognition through the work he is doing but still be dissatisfied with his work environment. Or—to put it another way—he can be highly motivated by his job but very unhappy about the working conditions.

Maintenance needs are usually satisfied through media that are administered for the benefit of the work group at large—in short, motivation needs are affected by individual job factors, maintenance needs on some mass basis. Maintenance needs take the form of such familiar features of the work en-

EXHIBIT 12
RELATION OF MAINTENANCE NEEDS TO MAINTENANCE MEDIA

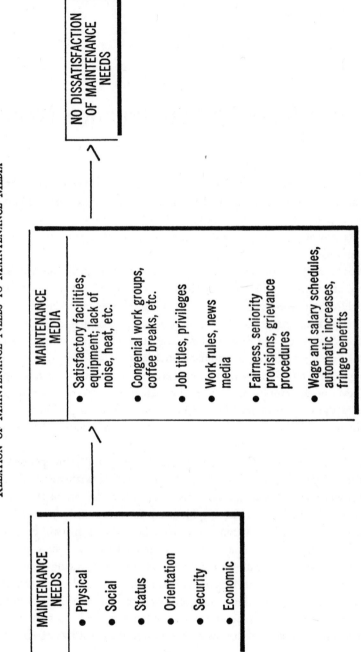

vironment as facilities, work groups, job titles and privileges, work rules and news media, seniority clauses and grievance procedures, and group-determined wages and salaries and fringe benefits. Exhibit 12 shows the relationship of maintenance needs—physical, social, status, orientation, security, economic—to such maintenance media. These are not the same media which satisfy motivation needs, and vice versa. Of course we must do a good job of satisfying maintenance needs—and American business on the whole has traditionally done this, particularly in recent years, although one can still find instances where physical or security needs are seriously neglected. People at work, however, sometimes misinterpret their own motivations because they have learned from society, management, or union leaders to try to satisfy insatiable maintenance needs.

What this means, it should be absolutely clear, is not that maintenance needs are irrelevant, unnecessary, or unimportant; rather, it underscores the fact that satisfied maintenance needs do not equal motivation or effective performance. Conversely, it means that dissatisfied maintenance needs—provided the degree of unhappiness is sufficiently great—may prevent goal-oriented work behavior.

But the evidence also tells management that motivated, goal-seeking people do become less concerned about maintenance factors. There are many instances in which employees express discontent with their life at work, and to which management mistakenly responds with more opportunities to satisfy maintenance needs instead of increased motivational opportunities. While motivation factors and maintenance factors interact to a degree, the interaction is one direction; for most situations we should consider them two separate phenomena. Managers too often waste company resources and fail to get the improved performance they feel they have a right to expect from more fringe benefits because maintenance needs are already satisfied. If they were to spend the same amount of time, money, and effort on providing opportunities to satisfy motivation needs as is traditionally spent on maintenance needs, the effects on company performance would be overwhelming.

When Maintenance Seeking Occurs

Maintenance seeking will occur as a result of preoccupation with maintenance factors, and this in turn usually results from (1) actual failure to satisfy maintenance needs or (2) poor conditions for motivation seeking. Poor conditions for motivation seeking include lack of personal and company goals, frustration of employee motivation needs, few motivation oppor-

EXHIBIT 13

MAINTENANCE-SEEKING CONDITIONS

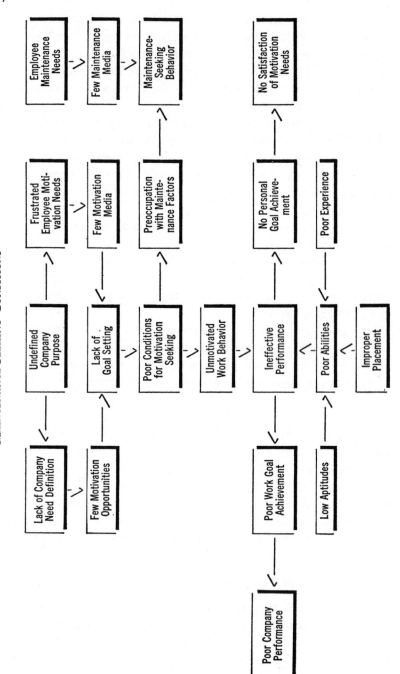

tunities and few media for satisfying those needs, and a general lack of goal orientation.

There are all too many opportunities for manipulating the work environment to produce maintenance-seeking behavior. In fact, if we will refer back to Chapter 16 and Exhibit 11, we will see that every part of the process of encouraging motivated, goal-seeking behavior can be perverted into an invitation to maintenance seeking. In order to sharpen our focus, let us consider the worst possible type of case. While it is truly a horrible example, it might not be too difficult to find such conditions in many companies. (See Exhibit 13.)

If management (under the leadership of the chief executive) neglects to define company purpose, it may easily fail, also, to define customer and company needs. Further, undefined company purpose may frustrate employee motivation needs. With inadequate corporate planning, with no recognizable company goals defined in a top-to-bottom sequence and interacting with employee goals, there will be few motivation opportunities and few motivation media. This is a situation completely opposed to the conditions necessary for effective performance. Instead of being goal seekers, people become preoccupied with maintenance factors—in spite of an otherwise adequate level of maintenance.

Some employees, to be sure, are chronic maintenance seekers from the day they are hired. This does not, however, negate the fact that management by its own policies and actions can block goal achievement and turn a motivated employee into a maintenance addict. If, additionally, maintenance needs are frustrated because there are few maintenance media, we achieve a vicious circle of ever-increasing maintenance seeking followed by ever-increasing attempts to avoid dissatisfaction with no way out.

And there are other ways to produce unmotivated work behavior and ineffective performance. One that particularly needs mention is poor ability —resulting from poor aptitudes, poor experience, or poor placement. The best conditions for motivation seeking will be of no use if individual employees' abilities make the goals unachievable.

On the other hand, we know by now that aptitudes, experience, and placement alone cannot produce effective performance; we need the right conditions for motivation and goal seeking as well. Without them we get poor work and personal goal achievement and, in turn, poor company performance. We reach an impasse in which neither motivation needs nor maintenance needs are satisfied and, since the cycle of maintenance seeking created by providing maintenance media without providing motivation opportunities is self-regenerating, the result is constant *escalation* of maintenance needs.

In simple terms, *management cannot "love" an employee into productivity regardless of what it does to make the job environment comfortable. What management can do is to provide interesting and challenging work by which an employee can satisfy his motivation needs.* And perhaps this is love.

The Maintenance Media

Let's look a little closer at some of the media by which maintenance needs can be satisfied. First (see Exhibit 12), there are the *physical* needs. These can be met by adequate facilities and working conditions—the absence of excessive noise and heat, for example, the provision of proper tools and equipment, a good company cafeteria, plenty of parking space, and a general environment in which dissatisfaction is minimized.

Social needs are satisfied through work groups, conversation at coffee breaks and lunch, recreation programs, and other devices which create opportunities for employees to meet with each other and with their supervisors in an informal atmosphere.

Status needs are satisfied by means of job titles and privileges, including office furnishings as well as plant and company identification. Many companies have a well-defined and highly organized system for satisfying status needs, but people often receive additional status symbols without increased status. In this case, the symbols supposedly stand for status but in fact do not. In contrast, status needs can be met through the work itself when the same media that satisfy them also become satisfiers of motivation needs. In other words, status can come from achievement of company and personal goals rather than simple "rank has its privileges" approaches.

Managers are particularly susceptible to the use of status symbols to indicate their importance. Large corporations may prescribe for an executive at a certain level the size and location of the office he is to have; the nature of the desk and other equipment; the draperies and rugs; the water carafe; the number of telephones; and the precise complement of attractive secretaries. These are excellent satisfiers of maintenance needs, but they do not produce or reward motivation. Yet they can turn the management group itself into the biggest maintenance seekers in the organization. Is there any wonder that rank-and-file plant and office employees grow concerned about *their* status?

Orientation needs can be satisfied through work rules, company manuals, and various company publications and pronouncements.

Security needs are met by all-round fairness, seniority provisions, grievance procedures, policies on full employment and layoff, company tradition, and union contracts.

Economic needs are obviously satisfied through wages and salaries and related benefits. It is interesting to note from research findings that economic needs are often placed in the maintenance rather than the motivation category. We can see why if we recall the characteristics of the goal seeker as compared with the task-oriented employee and, in light of the differences between the two, examine the way in which companies administer their wage and salary programs. The goal seeker's point of view about money has sometimes been misinterpreted by management and particularly by salary administrators to mean that because he often considers financial reward to be more of a maintenance factor than a motivation factor, money is unimportant. It is quite clear that money does motivate the goal setter, but only if it gives him the desired concrete feedback about his contribution to company goals and does not come to him just as a result of being part of the corporate family.

For this reason we conclude that money can satisfy both motivation and maintenance needs but that its success as a motivator is critically dependent upon the company's approach. If we reward an employee for establishing a challenging goal and beating it, we are using money as a motivator; however, if we simply hand out money in an automatic way and give increases without relating them clearly to the results achieved, then we are putting it in the category of a dissatisfier. Therefore, an effective wage and salary administration system must tie financial incentives and rewards unmistakably to company objectives and strategies. *If motivation is to come from the work itself, so too must the paycheck.*

Turning Maintenance Media into Motivators

Many media, in short, hold potential for both motivation and maintenance. But always the realization of this potential will depend on the particular company approach. Take, for instance, the pension that is given a long-service employee in a benevolent, paternalistic fashion as a form of gift. Because, as a result of this misguided benevolence, pension plans are often dissociated in management's mind from the achievement of company goals and bestowed without any involvement on the part of the employees, they fall in the maintenance category in most companies. However, it is possible for management to use retirement benefits as satisfiers of motivation needs.

To do this, we must apply the principles of goal setting. For instance, involving employees or their representatives in determining how company resources will be spent to increase benefits holds potential for motivation if the involvement is more than simple manipulative participation. Management may decide, say, that it is time to bring the company pension plan more in line with increased living costs. The traditional way of proceeding would be for management to devise the new scheme in secrecy without consulting either the employees themselves or knowledgeable and responsible personnel people. Management's usual reasoning is that the employees are incapable of deciding how the company's resources should be spent; if given the chance, they will bankrupt the company with their demands for more and more. Besides, word must not leak out to the company's competitors or to the unions.

These, in many cases, are legitimate reasons for caution. However, they are not arguments against involvement in company planning as much as they are indictments of management's past practices which have taught employees to expect to do battle with management over benefits. Furthermore, after announcing the improved pension plan management sits back and looks for improved performance and greater productivity, which do not come. This appears to reinforce the attitude that employees are insatiable with respect to maintenance factors. What it really proves is that maintenance seeking is prevalent in the organization—usually owing to the denial of opportunity to contribute meaningfully to the setting of company goals.

If the cost of a benefit is paid entirely by the company, management has a major but not exclusive role in determining how the money will be spent. If, however, employees share the cost—that is, spend their own money for their own benefits—management is offered a real opportunity for turning a maintenance factor into a motivating one. Employees who are asked to authorize deductions from their paychecks for benefits obviously must participate in determining how the money will be used or be denied an opportunity to set personal goals. Suppose management were to decide what portion of the company funds could be spent on pensions and then turn to the employees for ideas on allocating it. Since management has already decreed that there will be an improved program and has set a limit on the dollar amount to be spent for this purpose, the employees' participation will not cost the company anything additional. The employees can simply decide how much of their own money shall be added to the allotted funds to arrive at the total package.

These surely are conditions for motivation. If the company is unionized, management will be compelled to negotiate the increase with the employees' chosen representatives in any case—very possibly with such frustration and hostility on the part of both management and the union that the opportunity for individual involvement is denied. If there is no union, the opportunity for individuals to influence company planning within preset limits and to set personal goals as they relate to economic needs is not likely to bring unionization but may, in fact, be a deterrent.

Production standards are a somewhat different case. The usual industrial engineering approach to setting standards of production or quality is to have a staff group analyze the process, time it, and organize it; then the line foreman imposes it upon the production employees. Under these conditions standards are maintenance factors and sources of dissatisfaction or at best no dissatisfaction—certainly they are not sources of motivation. And we would rarely expect employees to exceed such externally imposed standards for very long. Because the job itself is the source of motivation that leads to effective performance, denial of the opportunity to set standards strips the work of most of its motivating potential. This is not an argument for abolishing standards. In fact, standards are necessary to motivation, for they enable the individual to know whether he is proceeding toward his goals. The question is whether the goals that he is seeking are imposed upon him or whether he has had some reasonable opportunity to influence how the standards which determine them will be set.

What has been found many times is that when employees have an opportunity to set standards for themselves, they set higher and more difficult achievement goals than any set for them by outside industrial engineering people. The difference is the increased motivation that improves performance. Where standards are imposed, the level of motivation is in most cases going to be lower; therefore, productivity is lower; and so industrial engineering sets lower standards in keeping with the overall atmosphere.

Involvement in setting standards does not imply that the supervisor tells the employees to set their own standards and then withdraws. He must of course provide all necessary assistance. In order to set realistic and meaningful standards, certain kinds of techniques and tools must be applied: work measurement, job timing, process flow, and quality control guides. Moreover, there are certain organizational constraints which the supervisor must explain. But many employees have jobs in which they could set their own standards if they were trained to do so and if they understood the goals of the department in terms of quantity, quality, cost, and time.

In other words, employee participation in setting standards must operate within a predetermined framework in which management sets the limits of reality and defines and communicates the department's objectives. Within this framework there is sufficient opportunity for personal involvement without throwing all work criteria out of the window. The Theory X supervisor who is threatened by people acting as humans rather than automatons may claim that work conditions and standards are such that employee involvement is not possible. Often, however, when the employees understand the facts they are quite willing to commit themselves to the achievement of goals on that basis for a reasonable length of time—though not year after year.

In summary, employees do not inevitably want more and more. Their concern with maintenance factors increases not because of the factors themselves but because the work itself is demotivating. They turn from the work itself to their environment and a search for motivation. They will not find it, however. Management must not make the mistake of trying to achieve motivation through maintenance needs. Neither increased pay nor additional fringe benefits will lead to effective performance—only a challenging job with achievable goals can do that. But involvement in the planning of benefit programs, in job design, and in the setting of performance standards can turn a dissatisfier into a motivator.

Chapter 18

Personal and Private Goals

S OME PERSONAL GOALS DO NOT RELATE TO THE JOB. THEY ARE NOT MET THROUGH membership in the business organization but are exclusively concerned with the individual's life. The question is, just how much satisfaction should work provide?

Personal goals that do relate to the job are the concern of the company. There is very little room for privacy with respect to them, although there should be maximum room for individuality. Off-the-job behavior is something else. It may be of real concern to managements, some of which go to the extent of interviewing the wife before the husband is hired. In any case, extensive investigation of the potential employee's personal life has raised considerable alarm.

In order to decide when a goal is personal and not private and when it is both personal and private, we have to look at the actual behavior of people and their employers. Many companies provide media which help to satisfy family goals as well as individual, private, off-the-job needs through recreation programs, insurance, vacations, credit unions, and the whole multitude of nonwork but company-related activities. For example, in the area of fringe benefits—which, incidentally, are no longer "fringe" and sometimes are not really "benefits"—we attempt to assist the individual in satisfying numerous off-the-job maintenance needs. The kindly corporate fathers who are fond of thinking in terms of the company family sometimes endeavor to minister to the needs of employees 24 hours a day and 7 days a week, every week of the year, even after retirement. Yet these same executives view with foreboding the supposed attempts of the Federal Government to provide "cradle to the grave" security. Rather, their concern with what they feel should be strictly private matters should be directed as much toward corporate as toward governmental activities. This is not a case of the employee bringing the company home with him; it is already there when he gets home, goes to the hospital, takes adult education courses, and finances his new car.

How Far Should the Company Go?

What should be the extent of the company's involvement in the employee's off-the-job behavior as well as his off-the-job needs? How far should a company go in providing for the achievement of goals that are not strictly work-related or are personal and private? If management does a good job of satisfying both motivation and maintenance needs at work, does it have the right or the ability to extend itself beyond the plant or office?

Motivation needs are essentially satisfied through the work itself; so there is relatively less cause for concern about this dimension. However, it *is* possible to satisfy motivation needs through activities other than the job; hobbies, sports, education for both employee and family fulfill their needs for growth, recognition, responsibility, and achievement. Maintenance needs at work and at home definitely overlap: Those for orientation, status, security, and physical well-being must be met at work, but companies sometimes attempt to take care of them away from the job also. For instance, we have had varying forms of the company store, company housing, company recreation, even religious relationships between employer and employee. How much responsibility should management assume for off-the-job maintenance? That is, how much should employees be seduced by an all-loving and all-pervading organization? Whatever the arguments may be, we are left in the end with one basic conclusion—that the individual, whether at work, at home, or at play, is ultimately responsible for his own behavior, his concept of himself, and his own existence.

Most off-the-job maintenance needs are satisfied through money—money that the majority of the population earns through employment. It has been said many times that money can't buy happiness; that, in the terms of this book, money can't satisfy motivation needs. But money, as the No. 1 mechanism in a free enterprise society for satisfying maintenance needs, will buy things that help avoid dissatisfaction. In other words, money buys freedom and opportunity—meaning, possibly, freedom from unnecessary or unwanted company (or governmental) controls off the job as well as the opportunity to seek other sources of motivation satisfiers and other means of handling maintenance needs. Individuals have personal goals that do not relate to the job, and companies have varying relationships to these nonjob needs. Only the individual can be responsible for the satisfaction of his needs even though on the job the company and its management is intimately involved in his personal goals. Off-the-job behavior and nonwork-related motivation and maintenance needs may or may not be satisfied through activities initiated by the company. Whether management engages in these kinds of activities is secondary to *the reasons why* the organization is concerned with off-the-job behavior. Perhaps the answer is a real and realized opportunity for employees to *not* participate in company-sponsored off-the-job activities, without on-the-job pressure to join in—in other words, simply the right to be left alone.

The Problem of Overcommitment

Another set of considerations relating to personal and private goals derives from apparent overcommitment to the company on the part of an employee to such a degree that his private goals disappear. It is not inconceivable that management might design its system for employee motivation satisfaction so successfully that nothing remains private and work goals leave no time, interest, or energy for other important matters.

All of us have observed something of the sort in isolated cases. An employee's involvement with the work group can obviously become so satisfying that membership in any other almost ceases to exist. Work can be so exciting and challenging to a person that he neglects his family. He ceases to be motivated by family factors because of the immense satisfaction he derives from his job. On the surface this may seem a conflict between the family and the job, but before we reject all our ideas about goal setting at work and lose the powerful motivation it can create, perhaps we should look at this problem in another way.

What an individual does, when psychologically or physically he deserts his family for his job, is to fail in comprehending and accepting the full range of personal and private goals that are necessary to the normal, well-rounded man. These goals must be considered in a context larger than corporate life alone and must include some that are related to the family—as well as the personal goals of the other family members. And relations among family members are subject to the very same human processes and needs as the relations of any other group. Our purpose in pointing this out is not to say that what is good for the employee is good for his children, although the analogy may be valid. It is simply to say that goal setting within the family is an entire subject in itself, particularly as it relates to opportunities (or the lack of them) for wives to satisfy their motivation needs and the strong incentives present in many families for women to become maintenance seekers. Work and family goals need not conflict, of course. They will, however, if the individual—by his extreme involvement in work goals—precludes involvement in family goals and problems; that is, if he refuses to set and seek family-related goals by a means that permits and encourages other individuals in the family to satisfy their needs also.

When an employee compartmentalizes his work behavior and his home behavior so that the one is exclusively a satisfier of motivation needs and the other is strictly concerned with maintenance needs, we have the conditions for dissatisfaction and unhappiness. To put it in somewhat different words, when a man is so motivated by his work that he fails to recognize his wife's and his children's motivation needs and to assist in satisfying these in addition to their maintenance needs, he has made a mistress of his job. For, if he is to have a balanced life, an individual simply cannot separate work from home and family and put each on the end of a scale. He must exist fully as a human being in both systems and not see either one as subordinate to the other. The job does not exist for the family, nor does the family exist for the job. However, the two should not be so intertwined that individuality— either of the employee himself or of the members of his family—is denied. Existence continues both on and off the job, and only personal and private goals adequately defined can help achieve the right perspective and the necessary interaction with other human beings.

The Entrepreneurial-Type Employee

We have looked at personal goals that essentially have nothing to do with the organization, and we have looked at their converse—organizational goals that have basically no involvement with the individual's private goals. But there is still another aspect of achieving a good balance. This requires that the individual conceive of himself as an entrepreneur.

Customarily, entrepreneurs are people who are in business for themselves. However, everyone who sells his services and talents to others is in a sense in business for himself; therefore, every individual member of a corporate group has a right to think of himself as engaging in private enterprise and as behaving essentially like an entrepreneur. He is an independent member of a society called a company who assists it to achieve certain goals and in return receives not only money but an opportunity to achieve personal goals. Instead of saying to himself, "I work for such and such a company," he might declare, "I work for myself, but I do it inside such and such an organization." In some companies it would clearly be impossible for such an attitude to develop or exist, but in view of the frequency with which employees change organizations today, it is apparent that many people have achieved this concept of themselves to a certain degree. They regard themselves as being basically in business for themselves wherever they can make the greatest contribution to overall objectives and receive the greatest personal satisfaction and rewards.

Obviously there are many entanglements—particularly in the area of delayed compensation and fringe benefits—which tend to limit the opportunity for a person to act independently. Also, management's attempts to retain key employees sometimes have the effect of retaining people who are not contributors and of making anyone who seeks employment in other companies an individual bargaining unit for maintenance as well as motivating factors.

An idea basic to entrepreneurship is the assumption of personal risk and responsibility for the results of one's actions—that is, achievement or nonachievement. As we have described the motivation seeker, he does pursue the opportunity for individual accountability and achievement and avoids being simply another submerged piece of the organizational machinery. The concept of self-employment within an organization is quite consistent with his pattern of achievement motivation; however, it is more than just another way of looking at one's situation. In fact, it would seem to contribute to improved motivation to achieve company goals. It helps to define the relationship of personal goals to organizational goals, and it establishes a true free enterprise type of relationship between employee and employer. It places the individual and the organization on a level where the interdependence of each is more clearly understood, and it avoids a relationship which obscures the need for the organization to contribute to individual goals as well as for the individual to contribute to organizational objectives.

Becoming more of an individual, separate and distinct from the group but not isolated from it personally, is an essential ingredient in the process of maturity. And the ability to distinguish oneself from the company for which one works and to realize the maturity and interaction of the goals of both is a manifestation of increasing maturity. In other words, personal and private goals are the responsibility of the individual, not the company, but organizational goals are the responsibility of the individuals who make up the company. In an atmosphere conducive to goal setting and achievement each person has an opportunity to be more than simply an employee. He can also be an entrepreneur who is not independent of the company but interdependent with it.

People, Organizations, and Purpose

Business has come a long way. It still has a long way to go. Simple mechanistic views of the world as a deterministic set of causes and effects appeal to managers who need to avoid the actualities of behavior. But it is equally absurd to act as though individuals and organizations had infinite options. Within the limits of psychological phenomena and physical structure, we must assume that our individual and organizational goals relate to a purpose which has value in terms of human behavior. If we cannot accept this premise, then our reasons for coming together in organizations become irrelevant.

Carl R. Rogers has written of the place of the individual in the new world of the behavioral sciences:

> If we frankly face the fact that science takes off from a subjectively chosen set of values, then we are free to select the values we wish to pursue. We are not limited to such stultifying goals as producing a controlled state of happiness, productivity, and the like. I would like to suggest a radically different alternative.
>
> Suppose we start with a set of ends, values, purposes, quite different from the type of goals we have been considering. Suppose we do this quite openly, setting them forth as a possible value choice to be accepted or rejected. Suppose we select a set of values which focuses on fluid elements of process, rather than static attributes. . . .
>
> 1. It is possible for us to choose to value man as a self-actualizing process of becoming; to value creativity, and the process by which knowledge becomes self-transcending.
> 2. We can proceed, by the methods of science, to discover the conditions which necessarily precede these processes, and through continuing experimentation, to discover better means of achieving these purposes.
> 3. It is possible for individuals or groups to set these conditions, with a minimum of power or control. According to present knowledge, the only authority necessary is the authority to establish certain qualities of interpersonal relationship.
> 4. Exposed to these conditions, present knowledge suggests that individuals become more self-responsible, make progress in self-actualiza-

tion, become more flexible, more unique and varied, more creatively adaptive.

5. Thus such an initial choice would inaugurate the beginnings of a social system or subsystem in which values, knowledge, adaptive skills, and even the concept of science would be continually changing and self-transcending. The emphasis would be upon man as a process of becoming.*

* *On Becoming a Person*, Houghton Mifflin Company, 1961, pp. 395, 398–399.

About the Author

Charles L. Hughes is Director of Personnel, Component Groups, of Texas Instruments Incorporated in Dallas, Texas. He received A.B. and M.A. degrees in 1955 and 1956 at Southern Methodist University, and a Ph.D. at the University of Houston in 1959. He is a member of the American Psychological Association and an officer of the Dallas Psychological Association.

Dr. Hughes was previously with International Business Machines Corporation, Data Systems Division, as Personnel and Management Development Manager, from 1959 to 1963, and was Consultant on Education Research for IBM from 1963 to 1964. In 1964 he assumed his present position with Texas Instruments Incorporated, where his functions include key personnel identification and development, attitude measurement, motivation research and development, and job design for increased human effectiveness.